JAY RAMSAY is a truly popular working poet who has contributed to many books, festivals and workshops. Founder of the Angels of Fire collective and the Chrysalis poetry project, he is the poet of the bestselling *Tao Te Ching* and a well-loved teacher, therapist and lecturer. His most recent book is *Alchemy: The Art of Transformation* (1997).

also by Jay Ramsay

<table>
<tr><td>POETRY</td><td>

Raw Spiritual – Selected Poems 1980 – 1985
Trwyn Meditations
The White Poem (with photographs by Carole Bruce)
The Great Return:
    The Opening
    Knife in the Light – a stage poem
    The Hole (books 1–3)
    In the Valley of Shadow – a ciné-poem-cum-fantasy
    Divinations (books 4–5)
transmissions
Strange Days
Journey to Eden (with Jenny Davis)
For Now (with Geoffrey Godbert)
Improvisations
Stories Beyond Words
Meditations on the Unknown God
Heart of Earth (book 6)
The Sacred Way (in Sacred Britain)
Out of this World
Midnight Silver
like lightning inside lightning

</td></tr>
<tr><td>AS EDITOR</td><td>

Angels of Fire – an Anthology of Radical Poetry in the 80's
Transformation – the Poetry of Spiritual Consciousness
Earth Ascending – an Anthology of Living Poetry

</td></tr>
<tr><td>PROSE</td><td>

Psychic Poetry – a Manifesto
The Rain, The Rain – a Prose Epiphany
The Chrysalis Poetry Correspondence Courses 1 & 2
Alchemy – the Art of Transformation

</td></tr>
<tr><td>TRANSLATIONS</td><td>

Tao Te Ching (with Man-Ho Kwok & Martin Palmer)
St. Patrick's Breastplate (in Living Christianity)
A New Version of The Lord's Prayer
I Ching (with Zhao Xiaomin & Martin Palmer)
Kuan Yin (with Man-Ho Kwok & Martin Palmer)
Tantrika – The Love Songs of the Sixth Dalai Lama

</td></tr>
</table>

Kingdom of the
EDGE

Poems for the Spirit

JAY RAMSAY

ELEMENT
Shaftesbury, Dorset • Boston, Massachusetts
Melbourne, Victoria

First published in the UK in 1999 by
Element Books Limited
Shaftesbury, Dorset SP7 8BP

Published in the USA in 1999 by
Element Books, Inc.
160 North Washington Street, Boston MA 02114

Published in Australia in 1999 by
Element Books
and distributed by Penguin Australia Limited
487 Maroondah Highway, Ringwood, Victoria 3134

Cover photographs courtesy of Getty Images
Cover image digital manipulation by Mark Slader
Cover design by Mark Slader
Design and typesetting by Mark Slader
Typeset in Meridien
Printed and bound in the Great Britain by J.W. Arrowsmith Ltd, Bristol

British Library Cataloguing in Publication
data available

Library of Congress Cataloging in Publication
data available

ISBN 1–86204–510–0

*for my mother in heaven,
my father on earth*

and the glory that is to come

My kingdom is not of this world

for he (the poet) not only beholds intensely the present as it is, and
discovers these laws according to which present things ought to be
ordered, but he beholds the future in the present, and his thoughts are
the germs of the flower and fruit of latest time

SHELLEY, A Defence of Poetry

The fire within you
Soft silken embers,
Is our whole duty—
But no one remembers

ARTHUR RIMBAUD, Season in Hell
(TRANSLATED BY PAUL SCHMIDT)

... for here there is no place
That does not see you. You must change your life.

RAINER MARIA RILKE, 'Archaic Torso of Apollo'

When a message has no clothes on
How can it be spoken?

THOMAS MERTON, A Messenger from the Horizon

I've read all the books but one
Only remains sacred: this
Volume of wonders, open
Always before my eyes.

KATHLEEN RAINE, Short Poems

CONTENTS

Preface

In a telephone interview I once gave on radio before a reading, I was asked one of the two questions poets most dread being asked, although it is a question I have always relished and needed: *What use is poetry?* And I found myself saying what I still believe: that poetry is not just words on a page, but a whole way of being, a whole way of relating, a whole attitude to life. It is a quality of feeling that is available to all of us and, as well as putting us in touch with what we do feel, it brings us closer to something more radical: our true individuality, as opposed to what we've been told about ourselves and what we are here to do. I have always said that poetry points to the most essential part of ourselves and that there is a poet in all of us, regardless of our contact with him or her. I believe we need to understand that rather more deeply without relegating what people do write to the realm of amateurism or therapy. For as long as we do that, what Adrian Mitchell said some years ago will remain the case: 'Most people ignore most poetry/because most poetry ignores most people.'

The second question is one that this book is designed to answer with as few additional words from its author as possible: *What do you write about?* I always find this harder to answer. I can say much more about *why* I write – and then I find that the *what* is in the *why.* As Jeremy Reed has written recently in his essay 'The Angel in Poetry', 'We demand more of the poem than a social conscience. We ask that it turns us round, so that we insight the marvellous inherent in the ordinary.' This is a statement with which I wholeheartedly agree.

In a letter I was lucky enough to receive from Ted Hughes months before his death, he stated (in relationship to my own work) the issue as he'd come to experience it, seeing it as something deeper than a question of elitism on the one hand, or instant accessibility on the other. As he said: 'After all my time at it, I'm beginning to realize the audience for most of what one might want to write is not there, even as a potential hunger for a taste still to be created. I'm beginning to feel that any verse which gets much beyond a kiss, a gentle handclasp, a caress, loses the modern reader. The modern editor, too.' His own work stands as a testament to what it means to hold depth and the intention to communicate simultaneously, and it is perhaps useful to remember that there has never been memorable or really worthwhile poetry without both of these aspects being honoured. For us as poets, that means returning to the source of our inspiration and commitment to what we are doing in the first place, rather than making the mistake of believing (as it is currently fashionable) that poetry is only a question of language.

Poetry for me began, where I hope it will always remain, in a sense of awe and wonder. It also began as a more urgent quest for meaning at a time when I wasn't sure, and certainly wasn't being told, whether life had any meaning beyond duty and a kind of vague sustainability. You could say that was a matter of life or death (for a fifteen-year-old such things have to be). But fortunately, for me at least, there was a third point: poetry. And there was one particular poet at that time who spoke to me, and it was in reading him that I felt something I wouldn't forget, although I still had the arduous and dispiriting experience of university to go through before I was able to begin writing. It was Shelley who made me understand that poetry was a great and natural thing, and that it was also a responsibility I was to find that had since been forsaken which (I felt) was asking to be recreated for our time.

I have written about my preoccupations at some length already in terms of politics, spirituality and poetic language.

Much of that thinking has helped clarify, at different stages, the poetry that is here, which I would rather let speak for itself. All I do want to add is that, for me, the communication of these things has become ever more important alongside my conviction that poetry offers us a unique lens for divining reality as well as transmitting what is really real. To do that, however, it needs to be able to go beyond the everyday and engage the other levels of existence we are part of: not only the vast realm of imagination, but also the awareness that goes beyond images into the realm of pure feeling, energy and 'light'. That in turn places a particular requirement on the poet – one that I have awakened to gradually and discovered as inevitable in terms of my own development.

And not just my own but, dare I say it, *our* own as well. Poetry, like dreaming, is prophetic. We are the instruments of its message which is the hidden and absolute story of our time. That story is all around us now as we increasingly realize. What I have tried to do is tell what I can of it and map something of its awesome territory, even though finally there is no map – only the thing itself we find is the pearl beyond price.

JAY RAMSAY

Editor's Note

Each poem relating to the *I Ching*, the Chinese divinatory oracle, is linked to a hexagram symbol, as shown, together with the meaning of the hexagram. These poems evoke the essence of the *I Ching* messages for us now.

Prelude: from

Psychic Poetry – a manifesto (1984)

Poetry is not a metaphor for life
                    it is life

it is
      moving through us
            sensually, rhythmically

it is
      an electromagnetic force

it is
      in us—so as to draw us

        into our seeing, so as

        to everyway sense
              our Living Here—

Poetry is poem is writing is
a divination of life.

Poetry is *the subject* through which:
the detachment of 'knowledge' and 'information' is made
self-conscious as a focus for the developing rhythm and
personal complexity of you your gift your self.

What a poet has been able to do in poetry now consists in
a wholescale transferring of *the poetic experience itself*

into life-work

        —it must be more
        than Literature
        than 'fiction'
        it must be more

if it is going
to help us
to live

it must break
its own ego-centred
surface, it must
break through

its technocratic void;
to embody its own breath
in the body that is
sound and air—

The World's Hell,
the World's Hope

Action

In dim twilight
White cold white sun
In the white sun
In the white sun's
White fire

a small speck
of shivering
shadow hovers

—there is no mountain here
no high tree here there is
no place here—

As now, and always
Again—now
Its speechless cry
And open eyes
As its wings die-dive
In the dark of the dark—

And into your heart's
Fluid and flute-fleeting
Then out—

Out again;
Still gone beyond us
Into its lightness,

Still   hovering
Small   so strong

in the breathless air

Dark of a Dream

Christ again and again

Christ   Christ   Christ

As an ice skater swish-arabesques to a spinning stop—
The rink in the stadium froze, hard
And Christ was on the cross there
And his pose was so embarrassing
And people were being sick, trying to leave
But they could not they were riveted
As a few more staggered across the sand
Covering their adoring faces in His Blood.

It was expertly made.
One matchstick: and a half-a-one: crosswise.
On it, a bleeding black dot

and a column of ants, marching away

Ystradafellte

To wake up, and wander out into the dream.
Crawl out of my sun-blue tent cocoon.
And walk down to the sound of waterfalls
Clefting the deep palm-line of the valley.

Handholds, and feet feeling firm on rocks;
To be alone, to feel the full force of peace
In the presence of witnessing this—hand
Trailing in water; and air, bathing ears:
Sheep bleat and unstrained chips of birdsong.

To sit, and wait. To listen and let through.

Gnats hover close like flecks of ash; and the smoke
Out of nose and mouth sets me still. Still enough.
A mosquito dips on the back of this hand,
And for once, I let it. Breeze in trees breathes,
Trees root earth: and grass roots: leaves feed
Back where sheep graze grass. And the sky is turning.

To be silent. To clear the mist inside you.
An owl hoots sleepily; and you follow the pool
As it trickles out and grows around mossy stones:

part and particle of a poem
that has no beginning or ending

Aloneness

There is a shadow
On the summer road,
Waiting for you
By every milestone.

This is your season.

Hungry for crystal.
To be—anonymous.
To burn into nothingness.

This is you.

Your slow, secretive
Inescapable growth

Becomes you.

And always the rain
Is only the rain,

Is only the

Is only

Is

Club Monte Solaire

This is a dead concept.

This is a plastic flower.

The hotels are high on emptiness,
Cars hoot impatient and glaring
This air of cool cool *ennui*.
Palm trees parody Tahiti.
And the heat beats
On lines of parasols and uniform chairs,
By the private or pay-up beaches.

The rich are not different: just distant,
It's a spray-on gloss every capitalist can buy.
And the day that lengthens
With absent tension
And dies, in the end, like any fashion
In a vacuous commercial abstraction—
The way the yachts wait like servants at anchor;
While the girls play detached, à la *Paris Match*.

This is the South of France;
But there is no spirit here—

The club is a ritual of smooth ejection,
An architectural wonder of psychic vivisection.

Here is your hyper-material future
While the gods observe their bored, cavorting pawns
Like Romans; from the sky.

Boys, beach-boys
Golden lads
In miniscule trunks
With bulging pricks on cocktail sticks,
Smirk, smile and stalk
Considering the aesthetics of cunt.

The Beach

Grey sea, sweat without warmth.

Lumped pebbles in a mindless crest,
Slipping and shifting a few near to the water.

Low tide rank sweet salt harbour smell.

The horizon is a fleet of rusty ships
Cheering their way to the abattoir.

Bunkers of rotting seaweed hair,
Blank unseeing eyes that peer and stare.
Detritus, dead wood and dead language.
Blobs of fish-egg, sucked little white brains
And the zero white sun behind a chemical cloud
Hangs above the Power Station, a looming
Magnified, mountain-sized

Skeletal shroud.

the price
of distance
is death.

Utterance

for Geoffrey Godbert

when in my true my primitive beginning/in utter retreat/fell
far into silence/could-not-speak…in that static, feeling-
illiterate/'voice' i had been taught/i was deaf/to this feminine
tongue, caged under the imago/of its impenetrably soulless,
self-protecting/intellectually sterile/immolated shell

without a visible nerve the breadth and length
of its stillborn blind body

—I broke down: witless, face effaced, abandoned/all the way
into the heart of my resistance/left naked, as if for dead;
to stutteringly begin/to try and utter

echoes, sounds, slow syllabic fragments/welling up out of
nothing/their strange music-inside-of-me…/drawn towards
the inner edge/spaceless, timeless/the wavelength the web/spun
stardust around the bruised/brain's indestructible beauty–

came in the light came through in colours came
tingling…upstream

to bathe in the balm
of its invisible expanse—

and came, returning, back in me, here/into the Human Valley…
its blood river/secretly uttering intimate unspokenness/in this
body's being

in a glimpse of our faces together caught up in it unknown

o you your rare smile your resonant laughter, All Of You

compelling this release to speech, surfacing/Voice, voices that
speak to us all in a single/sentence spilt-spelt out your hand,

curving onto paper, your hand scrawled/and spray-painted all
along the way—

where the heart is rising
your heart is rising

up to unfold in its fire,
up in this chant this dance of desire

where and when you and I can as we want to
meet and mingle and commingle and connect

Writing on Air

There is a page your hand
Can neither cover up
Nor ever rest on.

Transmit through typeface and meditate
To where the essentials are still unseen;

Reach space through these lucid dreams—

The page is air
Beyond this page,
A chaos of spring air—

Alive with signs that signify us
As images of complex force
At the root, the indefinite
It that haunts the traces of our lives,
And fires each moment another life—

A future written out on air.

Light

A dot surrounded by a circle.

The circle is the sky,
That lies unbroken.

You touch it, here, between your eyes.

It is working in you
A step ahead of you, once distant
And clouded, now clear and closening;
It is your heart's eye opening

Inside all the darkness you have passed through.
And the depth of that darkness you will go to.

Light, send yourself out in it—
Give it all you've been given; it is simple.

I no longer know, the light
Has swallowed my knife

At last. I am open.

Light: the way in

to this depth of ourselves

we are walking uncertainly towards

Light: these hands that touch
                              together
                                        in the night—

We Are Fighting For The Life There Is Left In You.

To the Swan

for S.

1.

Something gives, swan comes up ashore, I write
The word *awe* in the middle of a white page—
A window of tense space fading like mist,
Leaving this morning sun that blurs and then cleanses
Eyes that turn out content to be watching
Curtains thrown back to the sea, moving...
To headland and horizon—a line spread
Out of buzzing wakefulness: swan tipping her bill back,
To catch each last bright shaking of falling drops;
Drawing this raw world into the shape of her slow glide.

The open door shows a path and a leading on,
Stronger than a thin thread of doubt that hesitates.
I am opening this same door once more—again:
To take this journey that is being thought through me.

This is the path, and it goes to the sea.
And this is the sea and the sound that is healing me.

2.

Wind on cliff—wild around you;
Blown yellow gorse flowers—tossed hair—
Impossible to talk, walking, breathing in, lungfuls
Dive-eyes down into the sight of those amazing pounding waves.
Sound of air and water as a mirror
Of lightened storm sky, puffed blue,
And a cow behind us pissing squat-legged on dung earth.
This is the place, and we are connected
By spirit of skin-fire, voice
That utters us, as human, as near
And as far away

As a small white sail.

Walk on searching the waving ploughed ground;
Comb a useless piece of china bowl, and cherish a stone
Of fossilized, remembered earth

And tiny luminous needles of new corn.

Nothing of either time or date
Only chimes that echo…this pause
And evaporate, back to the yackering
Distracted ravens shading in through big cedars.
The dead are all here in the long shadows,
And we are given over here; the place is Roseland,
And there is no more God than this wild garden

Where a robin comes as close as two hands.

3.

Night signals that whisper on the air,
We are the signal here

Touch down softly bent down over our knees
With the tide coming in as each reach of wave
Runs out and drains, quick-quick-slow caressing
Of shingle kiss and tongue tip delved to soundless
Mouthing its body rapt bliss of us brings us to shimmering;
Silvered as stranded fish dreamily gasping for air—
Swim into a long lingering spiral let loose
Ah with that love, at length, at last, which breaks
Down our selves

Into this sky-sized open eye.

And the calm is a sea
Of flung back sheets.

And the calm
Is inviolate.

4.

Reaching the other side, reaching an island
Breast-stroke for miles under moonlight;
And the man is seated in a chair, bowed down,
Shivering at the ritual of his secret fears

Then he goes to the water's edge
Bare feet on sand; waits, and then wades in
Up to his waist; waits, and then falls in

Floating out as if dead, and with no direction
You found him washed up all sodden and wooden,
You covered him up in his sleep of death
You let him dream his broken fevers
Till the grub inside of him began to grow
With wings sheathed for flight,

As you stand; with your arms outstretched
Guarding the only possible
One last vision.

5.

And you take me over and you take me down,
Hardly knowing what I'm supposed to find
Wandering over the lush mound of green
Down, in a steep slope where the grass grows
Above my head, and the air is warm and humming,
As the path ends on a half-hidden beach—
An upturned boat, small slabs of grey stone

And this swan; waddling about, stretching her neck
Distended, beauty, preening her ruffled feathers, graced
Brought into what I am, and what I can't translate

There is only this crazing caring gesture to make
Against absolute nothingness: she comes out
And through this never-ending ending;
Wings raised up with a sudden croak
Up into their full flaring span,

And out of me, pouring into the sun-stream.

from
In the Valley of Shadow

Dark before the dawn
Stretched to the light's edge:
The green light ahead, and the black
Road that has led him here—

Pilgrim in the valley of shadow
A man near the century's turning
Brought to his knees by the roadside

Black clothes and shrunken aura
Black wind breathing between his eyes
And the weight of what has been
Still clouding his brain:
'God dammit, I've been in hell'
The unowned fear, violence and shame
The sheer body, the hairy hoarse
Stench he had to climb over
And fall to the end of his mind through
The dark that comes before the dawn
The darkest hour, when along the path
Came the God of Darkness Himself
With the pilgrim's skull in his hand

As he kneeled, and keeled over
And the weight opened in front of him

The poisoned river gouted out
He vomited paper and black blood
Slush of maggot, fungus and skin
Pulling the length of it
Out of his stomach—
The hell of the body without soul,
The hell of the heart without trust,
The hell of the mind without hope

In the dark before the dawn
See his tiny head and huge feet
See the weight strapped all over him
Pumped like a blood pressure tourniquet,
See his body immured in a mould of rock
See his clenched fist and bared teeth
His mouth opening, the hiss of his whisper
Croaking out life! life!

And he is so near, but he can't see
He can't speak for the swabs in his mouth
He can't hear for the deafening sound
Of the tunnel imploding around him
Of the unknown sky he is opening
Of the face he has seen as his own
To come to this

Chrysalis, in the stillness
Webbed and woven around him
Threaded with earth, grass and leaf-vein
Hung in a garden shed out of the rain
Surrounded by hands as the green flame
Gutters and stirs

In the dark before the dawn
On the eve of the equinox:
Cloud covered moon and stars
In a dark room, only trusting
The left hand's uncurling, unfolding
The strange half-formed writing
That it knows and I don't

And would sit, or stand
Waiting in this moment
Willing nothing, not even
The spread rainbow-winged flight
Before I am ready

To be born into the heart
Of the Angel of Life.

from

transmissions

I saw a great light come down over London,
And buildings and cars and people were still
They were held wherever they were under the sky's
Clear humming radiance as it descended—
Everywhere, in shops, behind desks and on trains
Everything stopped as the stillness came down
And touched the crown of our heads
As our eyes closed, and the sky filled us
And our minds became the sky—
And everyone, regardless of crime class or creed
Was touched; as slowly we began to stir
Out of this penetrated light-filled sleep
Dizzily as the hand completed its dialling,
And the train lurched forward
And I saw faces looking at one another questioning,
I saw people meeting eye to eye and standing
Half amazed by each other's presence
I saw their mouths silently shaping the word *why*
Why didn't we know this? and yet knowing
They already knew, and without words
We all stood searching for the gesture
That would say it—

As the lights went green, and we drove on.

The Other Side
of Seeing

Into the Depth

for Carole

Of this
Speechless closeness.
You cannot misunderstand it
If you want it to mean what it is—
I can tell—although
The words stick in my mouth, they
Won't come out; even
Inside, to me.

So I let them go.
I let all of me that I know go.
Forefinger, motioning my own lips to close
And then inching to slowly open out to yours, friend;
That you have filled my slight body up
To the brim, with your being, and it is this—
Kiss—as we cross over

Where our faces darken as one in the same space,
Tongue over tongue and into the depth
Of a darkness starred and streaked with flickers
Of breathing light—

Sky we wander and mouth this making love in
One unspoken language we are being spoken in—
Falters, searching for a true way for itself out here:
And at the same time as I turn away back to your mouth
I know it will not, where it finally begins,
Need to be written. So this is to say, kiss
And in your heart go through this—tear out this page

And take it, if it has reached you—
Because only the closeness can know, can ever know—
How deep the well-shaft with its water we drank

leads down to the seed

we were born to live

Knowing

All of it at once, now—and wholly
Within it, without tension
Or division—and always and only
Through having let be, let go
To come here, come clear, to reach
The other side out of the mist of our mind's
Unmoving eye—

Come over the edge of the sea with me
Come back into being what the whole of your body
Can see: this sea in us, and the wind blowing over it
As we drive down, drawn, by its strong subtle magnet
That is the love that we are, sharing each other
Inside it—

Leaving the car by the high stone sea wall, walking
Out into its roaring rounding from offshore
As the tide of it arrives with us and fills us, opened
As each wave is flung against and up—over the concrete
Walkway; spumes of spray airy as our steps move
Down like hurrying to dance, come on, let's go—

And we do what we both know, you smile, in your element
And I let myself go wide, jump and spin round—the sheer
Energy of it as always wordlessly and all-welcoming, us
Into its rhythm to translate it into *I love*, the
Inarticulate that only this body can speak, this
Unspeakable knowing that I am at last learning
How to speak—

Leaning out over the railing's edge, looking down into
This one wave's enormous curving trough, suspended, and as
It breaks shattering its foam-fall and is still, sucked
Back into its still always-about-to-fall shape—
As your eyes gone in swim in front of mine, and then closer
As your eyes become the sky's, your arms a part of mine
And the gulls glide riding the wind in your eyes
And my eyes move beneath yours and they are the sea—
And our breathing as we watch becomes the sea's moving
I find myself swaying: and there is nothing

Left between me and it, you and it, you and I: this is it
And we are running back laughing, drenched, under the wave
And some kids in shiny soaked anoraks go as close as they dare,
And a large shaggy dog bundles and rolls where the next wave's
Crest collapses over him, all one and at once—

As a couple from behind stand uncertainly in the balance
Of where the next wave is already rising; both hanging
Onto a bright blue umbrella above their heads—

As we shelter up above with the window wound open;
Watching ourselves becoming part of its memory
Woken deep, as now, so that every time we see
That it is all one self-reflecting thing—we are moved,
Reaching out to it—invisibly—filtering inside us
To the quick light living centre of what we are:

when you and I and the wave are one
and we are the sea

Notation

Space: come out here into the sunlit morning park,
Where the old gnarled trees stand bare
Among people spread and scattered out

In this place's opening;
And in breathing the relief of it, begin
To clear the head of its haze of chatter
So that the heart can expand
As naturally as the sky does—

Walking, loosely, down to where the ponds are
Ripple-full of the fluid clutter of living sound;
Staccato voices in mid-sentence, cut in with dogs'
Panting and racing, past kids' shrill screaming
Shrieks, and coots' bleeping cries; ducks' flap
Of disturbed wings, and a single swan's skidding out
In a slow white flash on the water—
And in the water, letting the eyes
Soften their fixed focus
And draw in the criss-cross eddyings
Of its trance:

Full,
To closing them, and to sit
Close-in to come into the stream
Of this continuous world unfolding—
That is each moment's note, and our note—the way
Everything notates itself and scores the moving air
According to its harmony, or lack of it—
And in as much as we can deepen to attune to it;
And bring the eye inside us out to see beyond seeing
Into being, as it is imaged inside each thing
As it words its wordless shape—

And we surround it, become music
With this silence, this space—that is

My body, your body's

Source of conscious self and wholly self-surpassing spirit.

〜

The White Poem

1.

Invisible world.

I have come to the edge of you.

Standing here, in my body, at ease, as if on air
Breathing in silence…

I have learnt to stand still.

Now the sea mist rising
                    a thin stream of cloud
Up the sheer
           falling away
                      dark stone cliff face
On the edge of where
               the grass ends
                       and the air begins.

I dreamt of walking along a line
I was naked in the dream
I was as I am

And to the left of my spine, my back
And one moving thigh calf and heel,
The half of him that was visible

Walking towards a sun
Along the length of a low broken boundary wall:

And then a little later on in inside time
I was awake sitting up on this jutting-out rock
It was cold and I was talking to you on tape,
I was opening as far as I could into the place

That is slow and which only the body knows—
This body of air
       this space from which words
Occur and rise
     to the mouth
         this sea of air
This body swims
      in its deepest speech into

This invisible space
       between the words
          white space
Sky space
    sky page
      the real page

And it began as a green disc of oscillating light
I watched it come out between my eyes—
I watched it coming out of my mind—the low tide
Sand and distant twilight headland behind it,

As it became the horizon, and expanded
And was green and then yellow and then white
Light being given back, into me, from it

As it gently grew huge and whitened
And was a white hole a white sun and in the sun
A colossal figure was standing, the male
Or female body partly hooded in a loose cloak
And the face in profile looking away to one side—
Irradiating light between my eyes,

And my eyes were open.

I call this the edge of the world,
We are alone here
     surrounded here
        as if on a mountain;

The path trailing off to the car park
And the cluster of hamlet houses
Their lead roofs and whitewashed walls–
The way you can look sometimes at something
Until it begins to disappear, its
Apparent solidity become light, the face

Of someone become featureless
                                    presence
                                            become space

The foreground fading
                        the sea rocks
                                    blending in mist;

As you kneel and peer down to where a group of gulls
Hover round one of the rocks split by swirling froth
And past the tangled barbed-wire fence
With its tufts of sheep's wool
                                    the cliff falling
Among scraps
            of abandoned material—

And out,
Over the edge
                watching a gull
                            flying out, apart

the grey mist white of it
                            beat by slow soundless beat

of its beak
            eye
                and wings

becoming invisible.

2.

Now enter this whiteness, where your steps are leading you
Back into that churchyard with its newly laid grave,
And the shock of suddenly all those bright twilit flowers
Taking your breath back—
                              and held it, bending down

Close where the rain
                    had smudged and blurred the handwriting

scrawled messages of farewell
to a dead man's soul
gone into the mist

gone into the mind, this human fleshed thing
become like a body of decaying words

gone out of the body into the mind,
as the thought the half-glimpsed image of it comes through

where we go through

from this charged place of him under the dug earth
on this edge where only the one sense can penetrate

to him that was him laid down here,
and him nowhere here at all, nothing at all

And as the waves roll in, coming in, out of the mist
Stirring in their white windblown crests

you come to the point
the point in my mind I reach
and ceaselessly fall back from

into the waves,
              the waves,
                        the waves.

3.

Something invisible in you brought you there
You came back, shaken, your tears blown away by the air
And told me. You turned from a trickling spring, saw it:
A great black cormorant splayed flat, its wings outstretched.
And then a gannet a few yards further on

And then a sheep with its belly ripped open
And then—your camera: jammed. And something unnameable
In you it took the whole week to start working through;
This intuitive fact of our being what happens
It is not fixed, nor is it random

But in that fluid space between, there, wherever you are
The place is you as strangely as you tell me your dream;
And that dead beach that haunted you was a mirror
Of all that it brought up in you, on the threshold

Of that dead life you died in.

4.

Dead body of house behind rusting iron farm gate
Open to the wind and to everything

An empty bottle drinking in water from the stream
Reflecting the weeds like trees in the undertow

And the rafters piled among plaster, and broken
Slates; and past a fallen roof-section, the outhouses

Became blended totally with the brambles, ivy and nettles.
Stairs you could walk up into the sky on—

And the sky, the thin blue endless abyss of it
Curving from the top of my head where I'm standing
And then inside the open walls, four square spaces

Through the empty front door framing
Under the contact sheet magnifier

your hidden face
only you can enter
and in the shadow
                    of what the earth is turning and turning
through
            the shadow-whole of what you
have passed through—
                        intact
ghost of you
            standing behind you

in your being that is living here,
this human ghost that is in shadow here

this valley of shadow you and I
are going through

this memory-landscape
                        dreamscape
                                    dream of life

threading out, as we talk
inside and out

of its invisible
                lens-like
                        beyond sense centre

that is light,
the image exposed
in fluent light
                moving
                        behind each image

wind and wave sway
and mood of face

tone of voice
                coded, visibly, approximately

in process
of becoming the evolving
point of itself
                in the mind's eye
                        the source

at flashpoint
trigger point and each line
of this as we are together traced
                    along the length

of its opened-out labyrinth
                  of outside and inside

and at their • of intersection
                  and across a threshold

that is blank white space
                between us/each line of this

filling and then fading
                each word of it you speak

on this air as it warms
                in its invisible ink white

and then vanishes,
is revised, is replaced
—whited out, retyped—
                begun again
                    in the mind's eye

the body's source
                at the deep interior
                    the earth
meditates and your mind mediates—

on this side of physical life,
as the road bends round and the stout open fence
borders the white sun's sea

the bare sailless mast of a moored yacht
heavy length of anchor chain on harbour stone
and the body deliberately treading the ground
and a solitary white car accelerating out of the mist;

and my body lying
                        down on the pebbles, letting
the sea sound
                cover me and the thought happen

thinking in white
                textures of white...

fallen feathers
                white sheets and the lines on this

cuttlefish, and this hand
                        and the blind touch

of a magnolia petal
                felt between finger-and-thumb

with the eyes closed,
walking, in step with each step
in my skin
                and the skin of you I touch

through the sound of running water, and behind you
as the firelight mounts
                                        in a time
                        turned inside out
                into space

5.

World visible and invisible
Become thought, visibly—
And in my body, my body you can see
And in my voice, and that which speaks
This voice

as the print rises
                    rubbed under your fingertips
up on the floating
                    surface of the paper

And if you took away the space
From the atoms within me
I would become what I am behind this image
I would become that vanishing

shadow-on-the-gravel,
                    focused in this illusion
of spaced particles
                    that shape him as human.

Midnight lunar aureole of light,
Crouching by the window breathing the night's cool depth
And over the surface of my skin

Beginning to feel

that closening
                    tuned sense that these hands
                                        touch
around your head
                    white figure, white presence

Distilled in skin, moonlit, bathing in it
Spoken in this clearness of your whispering voice
The sound of you in a being that is beyond ghost
Come through in its full subtle strength

slow heartbeat tremor
                    the stillness vibrating
                              embodied

on the edge of each slow white second's ending

In a square of white developed space,
Edge where this visible world of what we are
Enters into its energy
                    the hand's slow moving
soundless sound
                    of white on white, the traced letters illegibly
beyond me
                as it shapes and images each inch of this paraphrase

On the untouched pages
Of a book—a blank white book
Cover and each page I am turning—the whole thing

as I am standing in this
                        spirit body
                              Self that is here

From the body's depth, dreamt, drawn
Unfolding from its elemental image, earth—
Born bound and connected

to this air body of voice and speech
                              that is *I am*
                                    sunk
in the shadow light where each life
                              is being written

And deep in the closening distance where you have come
To stand beyond yourself in this moment of your mind here

gone through the body into the mind
coming back to flood the body with light

This is the sacrifice
Crossing the threshold now beyond all holding back

surrendered
            filled
                    as with you—

And the whole of it brought back into this mirage
Of our dehumanized suffering nothingness
Plane of which we are the makers and the reflections
Death of what we are dying through
                                    into this whiteness
of spirit self
            filtering, worked
                        consciously and complex

From within what we are invisibly journeying towards
Beyond this shrunken horizon of ourselves,

from this co-
            nnection, souce of our
                            extension continuing

as indelibly as we are continued—

Now it comes through as the sun fades to twilight

And outside, the silverlit leaf rustling wind

And in the silence where I have gone beyond him to meet you.

Beginning

Doing nothing about this
Or the day, or the time.
I don't know and I don't know
Lying back with the light behind my eyes
Watching the mind stop—
Watching my watch stop,
Letting it all stop,
Letting it go.

Thought-free, as the light is
As I drop whatever words come, one by one
Into the light's depth, the lap lap of the water
And a half-buried book left open in the sand
With its torn bleached pages I saw myself
Slowly scattering into the water—
And pages and pages I just crossed out.
Standing in the water and the water was light
Splashing it over each other and laughing
As we talked to each other with our eyes—

And now you lie with your face in silence,
I look at myself dissolving as I step
Forward to where I can carry nothing
Only the light of what already is in me,
Becoming that self as it has always been
Endlessly begun, and about to begin.

Sophia

To know, the way you know without knowing how
In the depth of your body where I would follow
This child's pointing finger to sense it, the way
A bird flies gliding to swoop down, and then round
Drawing these colours across the page—

To have the whole mind guided
Threaded through its own effacement
That opens it back out to the world
That simple dead world it thought it knew

You have taught me to dream, the way you do
By drinking the dream in with its strange blood
That we discover is our own: there is nothing
Apart from us, but ourselves: so I surrender
To listening and seeing every day now, watching
Each day's teaching unfolding, as you told me
About the horse you'd dreamt of filling the stable,
And you with its power, yours, to own

As he came to take you to yourself, standing up
Entering you, and crossing himself across you
To tell you that now, take care, you are pregnant
And then at last as you lay on the floor
And your breath offered you the drink and you took it,
As I am taking this—labouring, as you spoke of it
A moment before it came to you—your birth
Begun in your mouth letting the sounds come
Numb in the hands, and arms, head, turning
Into your stomach

To come out, spread, from your legs
As your tear-filled smiling, laughing self.

from
Trwyn Meditations

3.

—doing simple tasks
breaking off

kindling
from a pile
of dead ivy

from
tree clutch
grip
unbreakable
creeping up
each tree's length

till the hands
that freed them came,
and you
could feel
their relaxed
expanding

sixty foot
of tree-being
bidding him welcome;
their sap
soothing his back,
leaning

to catch his breath—
quietened
among them to each
careful stroke
of the saw,
and then

the pulling snap
of each
tough-skinned vein
cleansing his
mind of its
weight of cramped

driven fear
freed, here
in this homecoming
shared
between our eyes,
nod

no need to speak
most things
have a habit
of sounding pompous
or trivial
in this place of truth

the essentials
are all we need
—it strikes me
how much
needs to be simplified
how much
less said

when a nod, or that
kiss of our eyes
from fifty yards away
is enough
or sitting
by the fire with
the dead ivy burning

and my body
slumped, stretched
back
at peace
with itself

—for once

is enough.

4.

And then pain—
the heady cloudy—
red behind the eyes
...burning

:and it follows,
the way we are calmed
cleared, for each
unfinished business
of feeling to rise up
within us

—so watch yourself:
observe
the lack of trust
the old enemy of time
forcing
the moment
as the line breaks

in this forever
trying
to make words do
what they barely
in fact can—
and less and less
it seems,
as the years pass
and their
fragile autonomy shrinks
as the mystery
around them
closens and increases;
and the world
they are here for
becomes more real

so they become what they are:
hammer and liquid chisel
the breath's clothing
that each gesture
of the body
is constantly outliving—

so when you speak
I look for you always
at the end of what you say
through a glass darkly
and then face to face

from
New Age

In the dream, you said
You stood out under the stars
Filling your eyes as you slowly turned round
Alone out there in the dark that was not dark
But alive with starlight and your slow dancing
And as you moved you began to hear them sing
They filled your ears with a wave of sound
Sweeping across the face of the sky—
And one star you began to see
Drawing the sound towards itself
As it closened and brightened, you began to rise
You saw your body standing back
Your body rose around you like mist
Diving up through your arms into the air
The starlight star-sound you became
As the sky blazed with colour, streamed with colour
Flooding the length of you as you flew

And as your voice first came to me in light
Having died, you said, *right through my head*

I turn away, I turn away from death
You came like flame down into my heart
I sang your name out in light, my love
And my whole body became a heart

And now as I stand in my seeing
Under this open secret the sky is holding
In the sun behind the sun, eye behind my eyes
The sound comes down into my voice out of
That the living flame of the Word breaks through

We are the bridge where the worlds meet
We are the Spirit made manifest
Its essence the subtle form we are standing in
Reflecting the visible meaning of anything
In us, as us, and through us as it is
We are everything we have forgotten
We are here to remember and re-begin
People of God—we *are* God
When I say, my friend, I believe in you
Seeing your face in its feeling fineness
Feeling that life you have brought
Uniquely to light in each cell of you
Our being, freed from its chains, its dying
Is passionate realization—we have come
To live what is ours, to bring it through
And rise like the ground within us
Up through our hearts, heads, hands and eyes
This is a generation to end all generations
This is the place and this the time
And when I know what we can be, I am alive
I can see: we are the poem, we are its prophecy

WE ARE THE RAINBOW
SCORED ACROSS THE THUNDERCLOUD
WE ARE THE TREE OF LIFE
AND THE DESERT AROUND

WE ARE THE CAUSE
WE ARE THE SEED AND THE SEA

WE ARE THE FUTURE
WE HAVE ALWAYS BEEN

And as the scales hang in the balance
The building shakes as the air crashes past
Your voices eclipsed in the middle of the Mass
The wind rising in the bird-scattered trees
The warrior casting his arms outstretched
The healer's concentration unbroken
The child sitting silent and cross-legged
The hill where we stood in sunset silhouette

Let us pray out loud
Say it out loud
THIS IS OUR BIRTH AND OUR BREAKING
THIS IS THE CHOICE WE ARE MAKING

Atom…to molecule…molecule…to cell
Cell…to living tissue…tissue…to heart
Going into the heart…veins and capillaries
Arteries and lungs…brain and skeleton
The heart beat in me—
The heart beat beside me—
From chair to chair lined around the room
And beyond as far as each of us could reach
As I saw us standing forward in a circle
Surfacing to meet each other's eyes
Awed in the presence of who we really are here

Your voices become a wave of light
Breaking on my naked shore
A deep gold light where I walk
My feet in its ground become this ground
And all fear all aching thought all burden
Released in the clear sung calm of its strength
Seeping in through the pores of my skin—

And when it comes, when it begins
In a long horizontal flash like lightning

The Earth spins into—
At the moment of birth
Imagine
Everything gone silent
Our steps as if weightless
Our eyes without need of speech
Our minds pulsating
Our thoughts as one
Stunned act of music
Waking slowly from the grass
I am flung down onto
And meeting you
The whole of you
At last
For real
For this
And yes

We have come through.

∾

The Heart of It

Summa

for Snowdon Barnett

In the lap of the mountain's breath—
Unseen, unheard, unknown. The air breezing
Around his head, the traveller, the pilgrim.
His steps up from the valley he stands
Looking back towards: estuary and sands
And the cottage-dot among the trees
He has come from; and the mountain ahead
He is going to—and then rests,
At the foot of it—and suddenly, slowly
He finds the journey is all around him
Simultaneously: his head pillowed
On a rock, his body lying open to the sky
Feeling the ground beneath him both
As earth and cloud, height and depth—
Spreading at both his arms' length
And out from his feet, and his head,
In the lap of the mountain's breath
In the space of his empty body
Where the whole earth stills and centres.
The madman, the poet, the mystic, the dreamer—
He gives all of him birth there and death
Among the sheep, above the stream-path
He sheds them one by one until
The circle of his mind is clear
The murderer, the midwife, the angel
His arms and legs spread, his heart
The sky fills turning, his eyes, mouth
Closed, his nostrils barely breathing
As the light sweeps over his bones
And the earth covers him in skin
And hair and clothes, drawing his
Body back, clean as a blank page
His hand traces the unutterable
Name that rings and ripples out

With its shout of joy he calls
Into the ground under his mouth,
Face he kisses, friend he greets
Mountain top he lays his head against
And is no one, and everything, and is God.

from

Glastonbury Tryptych

at Chalice Well

Water to the well from deep in the earth,
Flowing down from the hills.

With the wind behind you, if you come here
You will find the lion of peace.

It is water, spouting smoothly from its stone mouth
In a quiet garden, and you can drink it.

A red gash between the yew branches,
And the well-cover with its symbol: *vesica piscis*

Let all our lovemaking come to this.

Iron strength of the water—
The arrows binding the circles together

So may we give as it gives.

And if the arrow is spirit, remember
Her face, sitting, grey-haired, eyes closed, on the wall
A blackbird's shadow flying by—

And the bowl of chalice water
You came away with in your heart.

A Fresh Blue Message

for Kim and Barrie, after Mozart

That bird's one note signalling
Blue light, fresh light, almost Spring
The shadows of the trees intertwined on the lawn—
Sudden, as always, unprecedented blossoming
Bare tree transformed—
And the bird's note like a mantra
Flashing its genius of light, given,
All of it, given
                    as he walked in the garden

He heard the whole of it in that one moment
Page after page, flooding the empty staves.
And you said, as you threaded a needle
The lacework began to brighten in front of you
The room went still around you as you closened
To the thread's entering the needle: hole
You entered, becoming the space of it
Then you were high on a mountain
                    as it edged through—

And as you wrote to the end of what you knew
Your hand poised, waiting, empty
As your eye followed your hand down the shaft of the pen
To its blue tip, till you became it—
And the rest flowed in invisible ink
Your hand followed, the rest was all there
As the rest of this is, unsealed from an envelope
The way the bird's sound
                    unseals itself all over the air

The singer sung: the song blazing with cloudless blue.

from
into the heart (a matrix poem)

Openers

for C.

A child stands in a garden.
You cry, and then you see him.
He cries, you have forgotten him.
You cry from a well so deep
There is no end to your tears, but beginning.

He is no cipher, but the real thing;
His face is your own, the years are nothing.
She holds you, then you hold him—
You hold him, and he is golden
He transforms, he conducts your wedding.

He smiles, he teaches you with grass
In a handful sprinkled over your knees.
He has answered you: you understand him,
Not even you could fail to, now—
As you say at last 'this is me, this is me'.

Parsifal

Purgatory. The slides flash by. This is where we suffer, but we suffer in hope. This is where we suffer for the rose.

Mist of emotions…and our faces in them. Red mist, and our faces gesturing, one by one—some grey, like smoke, some etched in splinters of black; some contorted, some crying… but wherever our eyes can meet, the doorway is near.

It leads up the heart's mountain, and it is bedrock. Red rock.

And it leads us back where we went wrong.

I have come seeking the clear song of blood:

for Gillian

There are wounded threads between us...see
They dissolve gently, although stretched
As tight as wires, strung like tuneless steel,
Finer than hairs caught in our throats:
And all the knots the mind made, tangled
In the mirror of both our distorting—
It is a hopeless mess, but for what we remember
First led us to be friends, that softens
Your pinched face, that eases my over-tense
Over-careful gestures—

We let trust take over, almost stealthily
As it closens closer than we ever were,
And closer still than what time has healed
Or could ever heal without us: what comes
Is here, and needs us: what I see is a heart
Hardened round a thorn the light as slowly
And trustingly surrounds, with what flows
Between us under our talking, and is the saying—
Behind our words, and these—

And call it by anything natural and it is
More natural still, more than we have ever been
Where the thorn eased out leaves a wound that bleeds
And then a mouth, a mouth that begins to speak
As we are speaking now: two mouths
Beyond the bramble-covered tunnel we plunged
Into, and lay stranded in; until the river flowed red.
We were lovers then, trying to be friends:
This side we are younger, and stranger than flesh.

Continued

Dreams, dreams as he rides—awake. Twilight comes into his mind, twilight-memory, but then as he remembers, it is now: and it is sweet.

The sun begins to go down over the heather. He shifts down into a low gear with a flick of his boot, and brings the bike up slowly.

And then, there, at the hill's top—the heather, flooded in amber, across the valley hillside, and a handful of sheep grazing, and a cottage ruin with its roof-slats lit up in the glow: then, there as he stops, and lifts the bike back onto its stand, and stands: then as he sees the light blazing over the heather…he knows—he knows that nothing dies.

He knows as he knew in the garden, and he knows this time it is beauty. It is beauty it is blood and it is alive. He is alive. He is in love. With who? With what? With this. He is standing in it. He is standing in it, and it is inside him and outside him and it is the same thing. And the air is warm and still and the sun is turning rose, and he can see to the end of his journey.

And he doesn't want to go.

Night, falling as gently as moth wings. Faces round a fire. It continues, as it must…and it sinks like rain, down behind his eyes, down into the ground of him. And one face reminds him. And then another. And it flows like the stream, glimmering and fading—and it grows like a well and like a hunger.

For one who has seen the rose, nothing less than it will do.

And if he is standing there now, he is reaching open his hands—and the light flows through them…the light there is no holding.

And there is only this: that his heart grows more and more like it.

Like yours, brother, gone now, into the sun. Like yours, mother.

And so he goes on down, over the hill.

Stitches across the wound.

His lanced genitals—

All day he goes fishing for the voice, but hears none.

He is a ghost to himself of despairing exhaustion.

Red thread among dead leaves, oak leaves. He could be trying to tie them back on to the trees.

Why these dreams? Why Stephen, in grey light, nodding on his horse as if frozen? Slanting across me, out of the sunlight? Or was it the moonlight… with rust on his armour?

I forget. I am full of questions.

An owl hoots, like a harbinger.

I have never understood owls, either.

for Chris

Moments later, it is winter.
A small bridge crosses a river,
And you leave the castle behind.

The snow white over everything,
And under the muffled crunch of your feet, ascending:
A small hill up towards the pine trees' darkening edge.

It even feels cold. You can see your breath.
Who are you now Parsifal? Without time,
Or a vizor to hide behind? Transparent man,
Your name, the quest's alone; and in you, like you
I could be anyone—
I am a journey that is my name.

And where do the trees beckon?
Inward, outward: all is heart now,
The mystery is both, and the same.

She sits, cloaked in a hood of sorrow;
Her lover is dead, you are partly to blame
Though you don't know why, so you listen
Until her tears are your heart's rain:
Then she asks you, as I have
'What is your quest now? What is your name?
What is it you have left behind?'

And all you can answer is heart,
The one word you speak until you hear it
The one syllabled flight, breath and soul of it;
As you say your quest is to the heart of life.

And then you see it. There—in front of you.
There–in the snow, its wings, the only sound
Disturbed into a low struggling and landing,
In among the dark of the trees, and leaving
Three bright drops of blood on the snow...

And it is there you kneel, as she watches you
Slowly reddening your finger in the blood
And lifting up your shirt you move it under
To trace its encircling, crossed, over your chest.

And who was the bird? But your heart
Your bright, your ruby thread.

for Carole

You speak your truth, my friend, as you always do:
But what was it you said that so stilled the air
Touching the core of this unconditionally—
The heart has its red lightning
That strikes through to what cannot be denied;

And you did it so cleanly, kneeling there,
Sitting on the floor as you reached for her hand
And looked up into her eyes to say
"Val, look at me as I am"– that one phrase
Gesturing through you to the whole of this:

It is a shield without a shield, a sword stripped
Of itself; become skin that is alive—
Passionately alive…truth-lover:
Look at me as I am, you say

And it echoes down time, like a gospel.

for Jill

You call yourself an atheist. Being born was futile:
All your life you've covered it up with achieving.
The achievement breaks. And now?

To hear you say the word *God* so nakedly: unknowing;
But you have come to the strait gate of the child

And as you speak of it—and her…you smile, you
Smile at yourself, and at the trust you find—
As it glows shamefacedly all round your face:

And may that gate always be open to you,
And you find your God in that garden.

∾

Humility

I stop and sit down at last
On the kerbside, with my feet in the gutter
And a hundredweight of boxes piled around me,
Resting my dirty fingernails and quivering hands
On my knees. *Let me be, let me breathe—*
For this moment. Nothing else. I open my eyes
And a woman, passing me, is laughing out loud
Her face tilted back gently releasing
The sound of it filling the air
And her grey hair, and all the pain she has lived
Lifts; as her friend beside her smiles
Step for step as they walk. Her laughter,
My breathing—out, smiling up through me, too.
It is enough, the gift of it, unwrapped
Unknowingly given, flung back like the pigeon's
Wings spread gliding in a flash of sunlight
Touching my head in a warm downflowing ripple-
Of-vibration; reaching my weariness to the quick
And calming everything—the street open
    For those few seconds that it needed to be:
    For as long as I asked for nothing
    And could only receive.

∾

Forgetting

My steps, his steps—as I stand aside
I feel the wind blowing aslant
And not a wind outside, but a wind within—
A breath like vanishing: thin skein
Behind which, as your voice stops,
Is air, enormous and silent and frightening
To think simply of the way I can forget everything,
Can turn outside myself that finished self
Before what's new can begin to come

And it's in that gap: in a dream I was cycling
Dropped handlebars, down, over bumpy mud-grass
I thought I knew, thought I was going home
Until I realized the grass wasn't smooth
And the white bar gate at the end wasn't there,
There was only the sky edging closer
Erasing the ground as it closened—
And the waking route was the same: turnings,
Junctions, traffic lights driven past a hundred times

Were all strange. And the strangest thing of all
The hollow sound of my own name—
As I became the wind, slipping through my eyes
Blowing a litter of images behind me;
Then I remembered: to turn and face the light,
I forgot myself and raised my head
To the sunlit clouds' white momentous moving
To the clearer than clear airbrush of the sky's blue:
'For behold, I make all things new'.

❦

from
A Bridge of Dreams

coda

It blazed in the sky, deep, soft, wide and white—
In the starlight and the starlit dark
And was 'the white loop of eternity'
Untied, like the outline of a mouth:
A great open wound of light, surrounded by stars.
You can look through the eyes of God
The dream voice said, assuring me
Speechless at its radiant simplicity—
You can look, and they are Love—as I gazed,
My heart answered and my hands gestured
Opening this channel of air, upwards
As I stood there

You can look through the eyes of God,
And open Him into your heart.

You can look through the eyes of God.

from
borderlines

v. zig-zag

in a place no way ahead, no see ahead/in a world like a
mirror in reverse/in a face struck dumb with questioning/in a
voice become a garbled prayer, remember—
                                    here is where we zig-zag

at the mind's end, where it begins/inside ourselves and
out/we brush shoulders and collide/here in this living

dream's inner seen/mist of broad eclipsed daylight
                    we find the line and lose it—

meaning? To find is to lose, and lose, loosed, is finding,
is found/profound? I'd say so/and so, the more
human/scoured and estranged to ourselves as we
are/one thing is certain
                    there is no hiding

and no exclusion/no laurels, I say, but self-renewal/and
who am 'I'/I know and know not/I am a clear voice,
and a chaos of feeling/I am a calm, and I am a constant
struggling
                    there is no tidy narrative for
                    there is no neat controlling

and in the dream you were floating like the dead and
calling/'Now is the time, but which way to turn?'/and
the way no way is in the asking/and daily, in the
receiving
                    the manna of understanding—RAINBOW

over-and-inner arching/at moments, rapid as a cut
knot, and slow as a thread suspending a liquid, star-
white crystal

as you remind me: of the old way of starlight/tacking,
windless/across the night waters/the ghost of the
straight line/dotted like road markings

and the road, mainly curved   like the rainbow   like space
itself
                    and the eagle, circling:

from
By the Shores of Loch Awe

for Carole

Before you wake—
Though the wind has blown all night
Before you wake
I would bring you this peace.

Rest now. Be with your dreams.
For the road is long,
But I know the way.

I go alone now. I have come.
To this place of the heart again:

And the peace is everywhere, you can hear it now
The peace is the bees, the peace is the flowers,
The peace is the flies, the peace is the stones,
And the peace is the man, sitting there

With the stream flow below, beneath the conifers
And what was rain…become clear, become sun
And the rain's whisper, a slow sea in the trees
Breathing now, as a fly lands on the page

And rubs its antennae, as if trusting him
The way the bee trusts the thistle it nestles in,
And the tiny snail the walls it crawls across,
And the toadstools the moss stump they grow on

And the far wall leans in the arms of the tree,
The green world is given sanctuary
As I would give it to you—

And the font is a well of soul,
A deep black well of soul,

Bubbling up from inside like a fountain
To bathe your face in;

And as you kneel at last, and see it
A voice like your own, but not your own
Can tell you
      Be cleansed in your heart.

Given

while reading Rilke

Not *think* of life, or *think* of death—you
Understand that it is not in words you will find either—
Nor even of the aeroplane passing, dragging the roar
Of the belly of its drowning sound…
Over the garden and the birdsong: but because
You have opened the window, and thought to let
The birds write their music on this page
In fluid streaked syllables of a single word;
And then the page you hold out in your open hands
Becomes white ground that weeds are flowering from,
And it is paper in your hands the birds are feeding from,
And it is manna your gift is giving back—
But do not even think of that: your hands are
Nowhere to be seen in the whiteness, nor the whiteness
Itself, effaced in living green: and so the birds
Sing, call and move freely: they eat of the page
And you joy quietly at their feeding…from
Your hands laid open, by the window that is open:

It is the Bread.

from
The Paradiso Drafts

2.

for Tim & Wendy Wheater

It could be as brief as this: that a man wakes
From a sleep of no dreams on a thin makeshift bed,
And walks down past breakfast through the kitchen
Door he opens out onto the grass

And still dizzy from sleep, stands
As if a little stunned, stands, and turning
Looking over to his right—is amazed
By the new morning sun slanting over it…

Blazing its dew light crystal towards him,
Dew drop after dew drop rolling filled with light
In a still sea of glass: and the grass, wild
With bergamot and clover, ragwort and camphor

Tiny purple violas, and celandines—celandine-gold
Stars in the sea, in the web of green: and the ground
Rising, and somewhere above his head, the sky—
And away down to his left, the actual sea

But this is, these are, the fields of light: and briefly,
In no longer than it takes him to stand like that
And glance aside: he is any man, he is Adam
He has stumbled out of time into paradise—

    with all the tender confusion
                of a soul who has just died

∾

4.

for Golden Flame

The sun, the new sun
Come through fire—
Come through blood-red
Come through the forgotten
Age of Gold: the sun,
Returning, having burnt
All time in its vortex—
Sun beyond the eagle
And Egypt; sun become
Reborn, radiant, raying
Shafts of pellucid light
Down against the thin cloud,
Down onto the sea

It blazes its late path across;
And the sun has made gold
Out of its blazing eye—
Out of blackness and eclipse
This sun has seen everything—
This sun has suffered, has
Drawn us through itself
In its gaze of open light—
Earth, and Venus, Mars,
Mercury and Saturn—
This sun unseen
Past its blinding
To its core of inner white

Now; as it rays and reaches
Over the water...
And we abandon the car
By the narrow roadside:
Walking over the grass
To the sea's valley edge—
To stand like breathing stones,
Lit, touched, flooded, silent
Eyes breathing closed, then open

So it comes—and the path's
Gleaming molten surface
Is like skin, rippling in...
As two birds glide, flying
In and out and in, across it—
To where it reaches and stops
Like a hand, at the limit
Of its outstretched fingers
And will you, will we, take it now?

And walk that way—
Walk standing still;
And the sun fills your eyes
And lightens your heart
And flows down to your feet
In our body's temple, this
Healing transmitter—
And gold, you are nothing less
Than love, you are naturally
Graced, all your gestures
Become so; you do not need
To kneel here, your prayer
Is a standing, your joy
Is its uttering, your face
Is raised, your heart
Is welling, and you let
Your arms rise—

And the sun pours down
Like hands on your brow
And the sun brands
As it opens you—light
To light, in what flows
Out from you to meet it...
And who am I but you now,
This now—and on this side;
The rest has gone, the rest
Is given: *not I, but this*
Light in me, clothed, nakedly

Is 'I am', is ready, has been
Bowed and broken, forged,
Heart-broken, heart-healed,
Re-moulded, re-cast—
This sun is heart
Is who you are at last

Ah, who you most long to be
And are most fearful of being
And can you believe it now?
The sun, as we turn to look into it
The sun is spinning
—yes, you can see it—
In a gap between the rocks
Where you put your hands to your heart
To bow, the sun
Is spinning now, first one way
Then the other—and how our eyes
Can see through its flaring dazzle
Into its cool lunar disc of white
And rose, rose-red, like a cloud
Around it; and blue, angel-blue
Smoking down like mist

This sun is a circle—
This sun is a dancing—
This sun is Alleluia
Like a raucous shout returning,
Laughing…and this sun
Is a deeper silence, wondering
What lightlessness is left
What pain it has taken
What sacrifice is left
Before we can begin
To live this sun:
To live the resurrection?

And the answer comes:
It has already begun.

The Room

The grey light, liquid across the windows, is a miracle of sound—of birds dawn-before-dawn chorusing, filling the grey with innumerable perforations of song.

The Night is over, and there are far more birds than were promised. There are hundreds of them singing. Hundreds!

Waking comes to a clear point. Something is understood finally, for the first time. It is the difference between fear and choice. And the clarity is a breath of air like mountain—a breath you could go the whole day on, whole days on.

One speaks, and I half close my eyes again. The inner form of the room is mist, where one writes at the table, and others stand behind him. He is in white, as they are, and then the window pales. What matters is their resonance with one another, entering through his back as he sits.

It is the same as when you feel an inexplicable tingling around you as you walk round the empty house.

The difference is that now the Night is over, you are no longer alone. There is no such thing as emptiness, there is only opening.

The birds sing. And the light turns silver.

from
For Now

for Gabriel Bradford Millar

2.

The landslide moves without a sound:
You watch the words fall,
Black into blackness
'By law of inner space to find
the real beginning,' you whispered.

And so you came into the desert
To find the zero of your emptiness,
The one clear circle—
The one clear, only circle
Embracing you.

3.

Fathomless unknown,
Behind and in everything—
Valley—kestrel—celandine
You nowhere and in everything—

And being nothing, being silenced,
Being unable to speak

You *see* every thing
And I see You
And I see I am
The core I am seeing:

The sun closening
To meet the man
Who has crossed the line,
Who has walked out of himself

Stands ahead there,
Naked in the light.

7a.

for Bill Lewis

Your gold brave shirt
And the blue moon rising…
—a gold, clouded O of mist.

9.

for Lesley

And the moon in the dark in a still-daylight sky,
With you, sitting under this oak—
With the stillness of the trees, silhouetted
And the breeze, and the far bleating of sheep
Up on the hillside;

The moon above the hill cut like a wedge of shadow,
And the trees, the trees alive in their darkness
And the moon the width of a V in the cloud—

And how much gentler we are, like children
Armourless in the trust of the night
And it is no longer raw between us
All the power we had is love, now
And love is the only work there is

So this time when you take my hand
It is hesitantly—but we are old friends,
We know that now

And we heal farther past than we can see;
We are healed, face to face

in the soft night breeze

15.

You stand in a garden
With grass and trees around you—

It can be sunlit and flower-bright
And it can be wild—your shadow
Standing in front of brambles, as if at twilight
Is dark, too, and you cannot see his face:
Your own truth is what grows from the root upwards.

18.
for Carole

What was the rain
And is now your face—
Clear, light, great eyed, innocent:
Your round face, your loving face;
Holy Spirit, you are a woman now
And she is you, here, beside me.

(after Cecil Collins)

21.
for the men

Out of the belly of the whale
Out of wrestling with the angel.
Out of the smallness of the child,

Out of failure, grey, and a broken flask
Out of the womb of your wounded heart
Returned to the nothing it seemed you were,
Comes a man you barely recognize—

Whose face is more your own than it has ever been;
As he comes over you, no longer as a mood
But a *knowing*—
        and it is him you turned
Away from, refusing to surrender
Even as you balk to name him: who else?
But as yourself, now
        and why?

Because he is a king.

28b.
for J.R.

Your burnt face
Scorched in the fire.
Puer of rage—
Narcissus of suffering

Your face is your heart,
Your face is cracking
Out of its mask:

Now may you blaze
And bless, and be blessed:
You are someone new

You are someone
You have never been.

38.
for C.

Butterfly man makes love with butterfly woman.
They are honey that wells from the rock together.
In the room stands an angel watching over you
He is bowed in light, winged in a blaze of ghost:
He is, or was, arms spread: nailed in red
And the wings he has now began in his heart,
And as he stands, he too becomes a butterfly.

from
Pilgrimage

for Sheila Holloway and i.m. Ann Wetherall,
founder of the Prison Phoenix Trust

day 2: Janet of the Foss

And as we walk back, the sign on the Methodist Chapel
Says it all, as you stand there smiling—
On the uncut grass, with its green door behind you:

> Live
> more
> lightly
> on the
> earth,

That I take as a message, as we follow in line
In a loose crocodile, crossing the clapper bridge
Because in our eyes we are all like children, thank God
Ponderous pilgrims, and children...

Climbing a steep stile over a dry stone wall
—as I help you over, Josephine, as tiny as a bird—
Onto the Pennine Way, and into a single-file meadow...
As we follow the path, at our own pace, and the land opens
Rising, to the left, criss-crossed with mazy boundaries,
Sketched in a pencil of low-veined Iron Age walls
Marking where the settlements and fields first were
Where the Fault Line runs between them,

And as we walk, a party of school kids closen behind us,
As the stream beside us quickens, and they quicken—
Until they flood all around us with their voices
Shrill and speedy and awake...talking names,
And talking about each other—'*He's* got a hamster'
One says to the other, as they pass us, oblivious,

And as we all go towards the dog-hole in the wall
Where the sheep wait, rounded up, and the farmer waits
With his sheep-face full of death, leaning on his stick;

And they pass ahead, on their journey, leaving us
Where the grass grows thick with dandelions and quietens
And the stream flow snakes slowly in among the trees
With its broad back of gleaming twilight water,
As the path grows wet with the thick musk scent
Of crushed wild garlic…tiptoeing round its edges,
As we closen to the Source, and its gathering roar…

And in a clearing between the trees, into an oval pool
Surrounded by stones—it pours, falling, she pours
In two splayed streams of white, in front of our faces
As we stand and gaze…streaming over parted thighs,
With two pads of foam below in the water like breasts
—and the cool scent of salt-spray in the roar of her—
And as she roars, she sings, this is her song of foam
Her Song of Water Songs, Janet of the Foss—
As she plunges down over the rock pointing upwards
Her water surrounds like hair, white hair,
White pouring, white-headed, John, as you stand watching her;

And we breathe, we breathe, we breathe out—
Wave after wave like sea, wave after wave of sea-roar
As it breaks and flows through me, as you do
Clearing my mind, all mind out, whiting it out with water

day 5; Back o' Skidda

The wind still in the morning, buffeting the eaves
And outside, through the squares of the window
The sun sliding in shadow over the grass of the fell,
My thoughts…and the painful laughter of the hens.

We decide on a walk—'Back o' Skidda', the three of us
While we've still got a morning, before we have to go—

As you gaze at a map tracing its brown-veined contours;
You've already half-planned it, and you're already dressed.
'Are you coming?', 'No', 'No thanks', which leaves us—
David with his rolled up socks and stick, ready
And you, Gwyn, with your Everest blue anorak...in complicity,
Because we all want to do some real wild walking.

The wind outside greets us, with fast-moving cloud...
The rain's still holding off—so far, so good—
And maybe the sky will clear...or maybe it won't,
What chance? The first cold drops are already starting,
But we're already committed, we have said 'I will'
And there's no turning back from the breath, or this,
There's no turning back when you've said 'I breathe'.

Reaching the long path turning off the road to the right,
'This must be where we go,' as you check the map
And I wonder at your rolled-up sleeves and bare head,
But you're smiling and your eyes are bright.
You pull up your hood. And immediately, the path is wind
Sweeping up the whole length of the valley it funnels—
Shrouding us in silence as we bow forward to its gradient,
Its steepening grey shale and slate gleaming with rain,
As we tread, step by step, under our feet...
Step by step, and stone by stone, as I breathe—
With my hands behind my back, the ground coming up to
    meet me.

Stone by stone until I've long lost count
The rain thickens, and we haven't spoken for a mile
What is this? Purgatory? Pure driving grey—
As finally we turn to shield ourselves from its needles
Turning our backs, exhausted, and crouching as if to shit.
Will it ever end? Remember what you said, Gwyn!
As finally we go on...until the stream crosses us—
And then the path runs out leaving us in grass wilderness,
And you're trying to hold the flimsy torn map,
The wind is ruthlessly tattering...

We branch up left, up the grass to the hill's edge:
And then we glimpse the tarn, slate-grey as thundercloud,
As we closen…all this rock become water—
All this rock become rain-water, like its colour…
And as we stand on the edge of its freezing bleak shore,
The rain plashes on its surface like beads of glass,
Hail-white, driven in wavelets, dissolving, bubbling
Liquid over a mirror there is no reflecting

As you turn to the Crags, to go for the top.
Sheer grass, the rock grass, with its lichen and ferns
And as I turn and glance, the wind-blown rain
Driving over the skein of the water like steam—
As I go back to my hands and feet to each slippery hold
As we pass the edgy sheep saying 'You must be crazy'.
They shift to one side, unable to run—
As the wind rises and loudens, bearing down
And as I crawl on the belly of the Mother, I think of you
As if I was you, with each fern in front of my face.
At least you got my postcard! 'The message is earth',
The message is you as it always was
Guiding me to fall in love with the ground,
But not fall here, or fall asleep as I could…

And then suddenly as we reach the top, the wind is treble
And the rain is horizontal—where are you?
As we walk forward stopped in our tracks, each of us—
Brought to a standstill where we are standing…
And in the cloud, cloud-white mist coming over like a veil
I can't see—I can't shout—it doesn't mean anything
As you disappear ahead somewhere over the brow,
Leaving us in whiteness—roaring whiteness—whiteness
Blitzing our senses, all at once, as we struggle to stand,
Until all we are is like hurtled rain drops, images,
On a screen of interference, snow-blind with static,
All there is is the whiteness pouring through—*where are you?*

'Where's David, for God's sake?', I'm roaring
As you shake your hooded head and open your hands—
And we huddle down to the edge out of the blast, waiting

'He must be going down the other way', 'Well, I hope so'
Gone over the brow into the whiteness
—and it's as if he has—
Gone beyond all words and images, all telling,
Gone into the roaring Breath of God, speechless to 'I am'.
And there's no sleeping on this edge, as we crouch
'We better get down while there's still some time'
And it's true, you could die up here, why not?
As you inch ahead, cold on your heels, to the bone
And I follow you, catching at grass, hanging on

As I straighten up and side-step—slipping once
While I'm thinking, *stop thinking*, as we go down
Leaving the whiteness behind us with its eerie glow—
For the whiteness ahead, where the rain cloud hangs
Pouring sheer over the grass and the scattered sheep
And the fields below…as we glimpse you, 'There he is!'
Coming down the other way, as you guessed—
And smiling as if nothing unusual had happened, the madman,
The sane man…or not quite smiling, because something had,
And that is in a privacy we will never know
This side of the Light, and of our faces…
'Thank God you're OK—what happened?' And you beamed,
You were much more than OK, much more. You were alive.

day 15: the heron (crossing Mull)

And as we follow it rounding the bay in a matter of yards
Before the emptiness begins again—
I glance down at a white shape floating in the water
And is it death, as my heart sinks, among the weeds
And is it a swan? It is impossible to tell—
It isn't near enough to see, but is the swan dead?
The swan song? Has loneliness died? Has love?
Beside it is life: a few feet further on,
Where a late lamb is suckling from its mother on a rock,
Pulling at her teats, as white as it, under her…
And between them, and beyond them, as you notice him first

And motion me to slow down,
                         quieten and hush

Is the heron: standing gaunt, blended in grey
So nearly invisible we could have missed him—
On a rock, by the water's edge, poised above the shallows,
Standing on his thin legs with his coat of feathers moving
In the breeze as they shiver, and he stands stock-still
As we breathe, expecting him to move, and he stays,
As the shallows move like underwater heather and hay
Floating as he waits, knowing his time:

Bird of death and life,
He raises his neck as if listening, twisting his head up,
To a sound beyond sound, carried from the sea…
From a mind we cannot think in, and only he can reach
As it reaches him—as he brings his head round
And looking down with a movement of his whole body
Brings one webbed foot forward, and then the other—
And then his razor-sharp sleek bill stabbing down, down
Once, as quick as a knife into the water, as he swallows

And then draws his neck in, to stand again
As he turns slightly, the air ruffling his front plumage
As if he can hear the slightest movement of the water
The inflow of a fishing boat covers, as he waits
Hunching back suddenly like a little old priest
Until it passes—and then, as he moves again,
His orange-lined beak parts like well-practised scissors
As if to speak, as he brings his neck back up
As if miles away, among the mountains and the cloud

And then with a sudden lunge—out of nowhere—
His beak goes back in to a square inch of water
In a flash like lightning far faster than your finger
On the shutter where all our seeing dissolves…

Leaving him, with his lunar neck like silver
Snake-silver, in a shimmering like light that isn't sun,

Or grey-shot cloud, or white invisible expanse—
There is only his presence, until he decides to leave
As abruptly
                lifting his wings, and flapping away

With his feet left dangling: his wings pterodactyl
As he disappears among a thicket of beech—
Leaving the shore like a mirror to gaze in

And what do you see in the grey of your own face?
'I see it dissolving into rock and water'
And what do you see then?
'I see the water and the rock
Dissolving into a sky that is my breathing…'
And what do you see then?
'I see nothing, and everything is breathing;
I have seen the beginning and I have seen the end'

~

from
Improvisations

Adam's Song

I, I have strayed far from Your Keep,
But I will return to Your Heart

I, I have strayed far from my name
But I will return to Your Breath

I, I have strayed far from Your Love
But I will return to Your Peace.

~

Light and Dark

Owl

You came out of the dark
You landed straight in our path—
Or no, you'd been sitting there, strangely waiting;
Only suddenly what we thought was a rabbit, stranded
In the full glare of the headlights, was you: turning
Your tawny beak-masked face to face us; there, in the middle
Of the lane. There, staring. There, unmoving.

And the difference was everything, the difference was
You did not move. You would not move. But stood, with your
Thick-set body perched, even as another car drew up behind us—
Even as the headlights dipped, and went dark too.
(In your eyes, I forgot for minutes what to do.)

The difference was: you had no fear. You said stop, and we had to.
And you said what you said with the whole of your being, *owl*.
What did you say? What are you saying now?

Only consider this: wisdom, or what you cannot name
That can stare back from the dark into the brightest light
Staying what you are, perfectly illuminated.

'Owl, you promise of darkness and of dawn'
You choose your moment, then: you choose when to lift your
Almost ungainly wings, and soundlessly go to a tree's height
Over the hedgerow.

> Only be what you are, be what you truly are
> And you will be whole, whole without fear.

Lines in Any Season

Lines from the dream coalesce and dissolve…
The refrain 'The poem is', and 'The poem blazes'.
Somewhere when, somewhere later
I bow my head before you, Lord of the Dream:

And even in this season—in any season
The sun as I sit bowed blazes through the window,
And shines, full, onto my face.

It must be You. It must be You again.

Transience

for Andy Goldsworthy

And the feeling moves on

'thin gateways', the dream said…pages of glass

                    —black print on cellophane pages,

The poem hangs unfinished
                              but the moment never does.

Or: snow-cut in glass

        —holes where the words were

        the words, holes in the snow-melting page

And your hands sculpting snow

Become a white sea around you as you crouch

And you walk in all that whiteness in your gloves and hat

You walk in silhouette and you are pure

    and the snow flakes around your shoulders like a cloak

Covering your footsteps behind you

*

Where are you now? In the intense blue of the sky

Over the hill of white

      where your clothes flake away and change

And blend with the colours of the Spring light

*

And in all this time, you have said nothing

Your lips are sealed in light and your eyes are clear
        living glass irises
Snow eyes of crystal
    pinioned like flowers

    melting down your cheeks like tears…

For Thomas Merton

Father Basil thanks God for making you,
And the world wants you for another guru—
But I know you: you loved the sunlight and the rabbits jumping
And you paced your cinderblock cell because you loved her,
Stopping at moments to add some more lines…
Wrestling your own heart for the truth, in the night:
And it's there I can come closest to you, seeing you
Stoking the little fire, or just staring into space,

Your schedule blurring under your eyes…

I thank God for making you human.

Hawthorn, Blackthorn

after Frances Horovitz

Bunched starlight   blossoming on the hardest of thorns,
The hardest of branches—

Where there is no consolation

As if squeezed out of the wood   out of the sap of sorrow:

These bright white explosions of tenderness.

Day of the Star

All night the voyage back to you, with the engine sound still
ringing in my ears.

And then you opened the covers of the bed, and I came to
you without a word
     …and your belly glowed white in the dark.

Star, star shimmering at our apex

And now we wake with the whiteness between us that has
come from this.

There is no mind to dissect or discuss.

Everything is left hanging.

We are letting the star do its work.

It is the highest in us

It flows in my blood, and is clear behind my eyes; and it is
neither of these, but around me, inside me...

Smiling at you, at peace with you, how so, strangely.

And You are with us, and in us.

Because I have no words, and I don't want to talk. Any talking
would be *out* of here and even the thought of it is a strain—

But you say we look translucent, and you are right.

It is a cloak of light around us, and nothing could be more
human.

And I can smile at you in the rightness, and it is enough.

Or we can hold and touch each other, and we do.

And it is silent, this new Love.

It is silent in our cells like snow.

The Stone

I suppose it would be you, showing me the *alchemilla*
That caught my wordless eye with its pearls of rain
It held on the pale green skin of its leaves
And cupped in their centres—that was the water

They used, you said…its taste, sweeter than rain
Licked off the end of one finger
(And the white flowers of the Seal winking nearby)

And I suppose it would be like this, digging
Stone after stone up with a fork
Under the grass turf and the parchment nettle roots:
Old chips from the house, and bricks, some halved,
Some whole, some burnt with blackened edges
—like summits, but downwards: of course, 'down'—
Before coming to the stone,

Or rather, one that wouldn't come up—struck
With the side of the gouging spade like the others,
But deeper: and despite being dug round, still not budging—
I suppose it would have to be like this, buried in the earth
Deeper than the rest, and treated like them—
Until I bend down rubbing it clear with a finger
And there, near its upper edge is its strange inverted S
Curled like two snakes that changes it instantly,

That goes on digging round it, but carefully, slowly
That says, without saying it, *you can take as long as you like now:*
To think of you, buried under there for so long
Charged with the energy of the ground
To be brought back, brought up like a trophy—
Or else say it's just a slightly unusual stone,
And nothing to you, maybe:
But it's good enough for me.

It Goes On (Chiron III)

Is evil here to stay?

Rain-mist on the window panes, and wind, waking—
Grey aching light the sun has dropped into.
The draught-gaps in the house breathe with cold air,

And the loose metal panel high on the side barn starts banging.

The wind soughs, set for hours, as the year circles
And all the darkness in the world is in one person,
One man struggling in deep waters towards birth.
His shadow flickers down through the months as if deep
    under the earth.

The first shot's fired—and no, it's not a crop scarer.
Black figures line the high field etched against the green, erect.
The birds fall, or scatter sideways, and in the next-door field
The heifers kneel down and wait for the rain.

They tramp the furrows, as they trample, firing—
And they hack in winter before the leaves have even left the trees.

And yes, it goes on, it's not over yet, or even begun:
It goes on—until the wound is open in everyone.

You are a River and a Rose

for Virginia, long distance

The past is bleeding
And as you speak of it, and speak it
It frightens you to speak: your truth, your beauty

You are a river and a rose.
I'm thinking it, but not saying it yet
But I'm feeling it from where you fear to feel—
As you read to me from letters you've never sent
And things you've never said out loud,
And you are a river and a rose: I'll say it now

Your wound is your gift, and your wound your healing
And with no ring on your finger, you are naked, open—

Sitting by that fire with its glow on your face
As you meet my eyes, without words then, as now
Or now, like a stammering.

So, speak them now (as you talk on, talk on)
And you do —you say some in Italian—
And they sing like the river as they blossom open,
And time is no distance…and the years are nothing,
The fire is glowing on your face like a blush—

And you are bleeding, and your heart is grieving:
And you are a river and a rose
And you are breathing, and your heart is open;
And you are a river and a rose.

~

from the
Tao Te Ching

in memoriam Ted Partridge

What holds, what you can trust
Is the same as this quietness—
And it is light-hearted.

This quiet light-hearted silence
Is the key to being free from emotion.

The sage never abandons the Tao,
He never lets its weight out of his sight.

He may live in a fabulous house
But he never gets caught up wanting to—

And though there are always temptations,
He stays unswayed, and smiles.

So why is it that our rulers
Seem so bright, but are
Glib and insubstantial?

Losing the weight of the Tao
Means you lose your root;

And when you can't sit still
You lose
      the source.

Translated with Man-Ho Kwok and Martin Palmer

On an Icon of St. John

for Martin Palmer

What gleams is the gold, rough-hewn around him,
As if emanating from him—

All that his face and being have been through,
All that desert and crucifixion
Has left him clear, clean and wild like You
With his straggling hair and matted beard.
And deep green olive robe…

And as he leans his head to the right to regard you,
He gestures with his hands: one raised, one down
And he doesn't open his mouth, he says it with his eyes:
'The way up is the way down
I will raise you, and as you rise you will descend'
And it is You who is saying it then—
As the ruby red halo around his throat and crown knows.

Mother Song

for C., after Mother Meera

Waters break
Waters deep,
Time my child
Time, my child

All that's hurt
All that's lost
Will find itself
Will find its source

Soften, soften
Only open
Soften, soften
Flow like the breeze

I am with you,
I am in you
In every branch
And every creature

Lie down my child and sleep
Lie down by this stream

Waters break
Waters deep,
Time my child
Time, my child

I will hold you
I will heal you
When you see
You are in Me.

Prayer at Sheepscombe

Spirit of the wind
Breathe down over these valleys,

Spirit of the air
Breathe in our blood,

Spirit of the water
Cleanse our eyes,

Spirit of the earth
Warm our feet,

Spirit of fire
Penetrate our hearts—

Spirit of fire
Enter our minds—

Spirit of fire
Strengthen our seeing—

That we may walk in truth
On Your Living Ground.

Fragment on Swift's Hill

White flame of leaves
                                        at the base
Signalling this place:

—a raucous crow flapping away to the left—

And the O of the hill

Up its worn thread of path

    Rising under the daylight moon

Like a pencil-thin sketch in the blue:

And the green carpeted in cowslips,
Standing on their tall stems
                  trumpeting yellow

And mauve, their mauve small companions
On this steep edge of grass—

And these are the new flowers, the rare ones,
These are the paradise flowers, saying
'We have come now'
                abundant as mushrooms

'We are the New Earth rising'—
Their sunlit yellowness stunned-to
As fragile as the breeze stirring them, staunch yellow
As primroses—but look—upstanding,
                    vertical

Speaking truly of the love
      —not romance down the lane—
But something stronger and harder to stand for
Now, in its name

And in the valley below, all the valleys rising
The beeches tall in their leaved green, and silent
As an army, a phalanx massed behind me
                    as I stand

And breathe with them at my back
Rising in their sap like spines…

'Stand now' they are saying, 'stand now'
And like the whole of the silent world, they know

That now is the time or never, and there is no other—

Now, by these steps
                          now, in this afternoon light

As the very ground yields up this rising
Out of the dew-moist green of its skin

Like a woman's eyes shining with love that is fire
Rage, like yours, as you stare and blaze silently—

And its blossom can only be tenderness, too, rose
Can only be as these petals in the breeze

                              fluted clean in the light
As you know...

Can only be life like a mouth without words
That has only its sensual being, giving its all—

That is its, is their, silencing shout

That is the earth's whole shout
                          ringing across the world.

Love's Way

Koan

for K.

No mind   no mind
No mind   no mind

Only heart
         only trust
                 only touch

from
Stories Beyond Words

for K.

And as we sat outside on the grass I saw how much we bring
to each other.

And when there is nothing left, and nothing between us,
there is only this silence that is the brightness of your eyes.

And I could have been saying 'You mean, that...' asking you,
and all your answer was yes.

And the blue of the sky was above your face and around it, as
I lay back—I was laid back down.

And I did not know who you were or who I was.

I only knew this, and that you were this, and I was this, and it
was the same.

And I didn't know words, I only knew your face, suddenly
and completely in the deepening twilight.

I knew it, and there was no time.

And the blue of the sky became dark before we moved.

We sat up and stood, side by side; and we were one with each other.

We were one silent ineffable mind.

In the End: The Beginning

for Kim Simpson

There is something in the end there is no avoiding
That is more present than breath, than self, than distraction
More present than this moment? Yes, even that—

Even than all those birds perched high in the Tree of Heaven,
That broke into all your wondering—even than
That huge exotic shrine at the centre of your heart,
Your voice, your whole face turned inward…
Or mine now—as I cut it back, back
From my thoughts: to my being; then my breath
And then, not even that

And across the gulf of silence from before
Names, images—before whiteness was even born—
And now, at the heart of emptiness
Where there is no I, no breathing even
Or only this suspended pause

'There is only Love that made us, only Love'
And You in the vast silence like an ocean without water,
Like rain before rain—
      like an unbroken mirror

You in the Womb of Love.

from
At Glasshampton Monastery

Solitude

In the high square window of a tower room
A monk is dancing—*dancing*?
　　　　　　　　　　as I glance up
At his silhouette passing framed by the window behind him;
And he is—he is dancing…as the wind pauses
In silence under the grey-still-unbrightening-sky,

As I wonder what music he's listening to
Is it rock 'n' roll, reggae, Salsa or what?

And it is him, him with the brown face
Grinning briefly out of his contemplation,
Alone with himself, with only God watching him
Dancing…and then pausing, pacing,

And maybe dancing to silence and speaking out loud,
Or praying (as he passes the lit squares again)

And who am I to say? He could be saying
'It's all a dance, man, in love or fear or pain.'

Reflection

'who taketh away the sins of the world'

W*hy is it, Lamb-like,*
You take away all power of speech?
You take all souls into Yourself—
Into Your Whiteness that is ours, and naked
Deep within our secret selves
And then You give us back our gifts.

And they are not to be what we will, but are:
And what we've always been before the world
And what we brought here from You, in You
Before we knew Your Name.

Radiant child,
With his face like a sun
Full of warmth and love!
Gold before gold, gold before the wounding,
Gold of pure light.

You gave me back my eyes, my smile—
Whatever I asked for
You gave me back my face
That is one with what it sees and feels,
You gave me back my life

You gave it back to me to give it, now
As freely as You gave it
So that in its eye-bright smiling
I would always find You

Lamb of smiling light—

And I would find all You found
In answering faces and hard faces
That stoned you with their coldness, and passed on by

How you ask me now
To carry a cross
Made of light:

Christ-child, my Christ.

Through the Wicklow Gap

The mountains beyond swelling in dream,
Patterned with furze and rich dark green in the light
Moving over them in silence, like cloud, unclouded;
And the foreground harsh: a field ploughed among boulders,
Outsized, littering the sides of the furrows…
And on the other side of the road, cattle grazing –
One licking at a stone for a mouthful of grass: none—

Gorse that could be Cornwall, pines that could be Scotland;
Everything reminding us of elsewhere, that is Ireland
Elsewhere and other, taken all together—
Blended like a patchwork of memories that become this:
And the sky ('But the sky', you say) is open,
And so much more open…as the mountains rise to meet it,
And the cloud flecks seahorse-white dancing them all round,

And we are clattering along in bright bold yellow, and dreaming
And as the gap descends, like a gorge into its crevice
A thin stone tower like a pencil stands sheer
And sharpened above gravestones, tree-tops, and walkers
At Glendalough: where a young lad in full cycling gear
Stands on a little bridge, gazing and gazing into the stream,
As we stand with him, without speaking, in awe of him—

And the lake below is a daydream in silver, under a plunging slope
Where the whole air ripples from the first invisible stone
And by the water's edge, one curled like a ram asleep
Is surrounded by eddying…and as I sit and dream the moon-day
There is a wishing well under us as we sit, we three,
And we are drawing up from the silver water what we will
As our pieces of silver sink. *Safe home, in the heart of it.*

from
At Cortijo Romero

Night and Day

Night, the start—Orion splayed above the valley
With his belt and his sword-tip hanging down,
Night, the burning—the electricity station
Lit like a skeleton dead centre in raw light
And the music blaring from a solitary bar,
And the football cheers from distant houses.

Night, the cicadas hissing their dry squeal
On the road we walked, and the rubbish dump smouldering,
Smoke from the low centre under bones of light

Night, the unappeasable passion
Of your dolled-up blonde hair and electric smooth thighs.

Daylight washes the landscapes in light,
Waking like monks high on the mountain
Greeting the day of God
Like a blanket of brightness over every contour:
Green slope-side under blue, etched
Its descending right-angle path
The bright cream unlit facade of the houses
And the plain of olives that are green-silver,
Silver as birches, as the light mixes with them.

Birds startle and dip, one blackly over me—
Over my head like a boomerang
As they chirrup their high jazz in a far-up octave
Of free sound and free-hand.

Frog's belch still waking
Dreaming below in the pools—
Dogs, and a cockerel: the all day dawn chorus
Of birds and engines: the day's work grinding.

Light descends into sound—
Only the inbreath and outbreath stays like the air
And if you sit still long enough
You will be like the sun holding the earth in infinity
Fused with every living thing that is and moves
Like a consummation reaching from your head into your body
The way the sky soaks into the ground like its lover,
Its visible body, the Sierra of Orgiva.

And he saw that it was good.

Desert Rose

Inexplicably, miraculously, as you tell me what it is
(How could sun-blazed shifting sand
Create any flower, let alone a rose?)
Until I hold it in my palm, and I see
The pain, not the petals, that has made it—
The layers overlapping like warts on raw skin
Under a foreskin drawn back, abruptly remind me—
Before the flaps become petals again, opening

And then I wonder what moment of sand could make this?
What tension, what intense unimaginable happening
In the cells struck by light—what rainless rain,
What heartbeat inside the rock where no heart is
Or no visible heart, only heat

And the ground, pummelled by light, responding
With a mute flower that not even the sun could see
Blind to its blinding?

Rock rose, desert rose, you prove
That the earth is heart, every inch of it—
And that the heart is the earth's response to light
Every moment of it—
And now you flower where nothing is supposed to flower,

Or can flower—you do it: you blossom
You sculpt the skin of the sand as you stretch like a lover,
And you teach me the hardest heart is all secret blossoming

And if you were all that was left of the earth
All I had to carry to a distant star—
They would look at you, amazed; and I would be proud.

At O-Sel-Ling

Nothing could be simpler or more real than this:
The air, as clear as breath, and so fresh and still
And silent, because nothing needs to be said—
Everything is so clearly itself, and in place,
As you walk on ahead up the narrow worn path…
It is understood as it is: these stone-built huts
Perched on the mountain's edge, these vegetable plots;
And as I glance down, a single light-brown cow grazing
Like the only one of its kind, on a long white rope…
Everything is cared for as it is—nothing is wasted,
And there's no need to do anything but breathe, and be, and live.

The Way Through

for Kim

Your hand your last gift to me
With the loving clear crystal of your voice
As I ask you 'How can we live past our karma?'
And you say it at once—*see through it*
See through it like a window in front of you
—this window of air and the lawn we glance over—
And though it will always be with you
(Son of Man, like your own true cross)

Here, now, is where you can be free of it
Free to stand in your Self as you are…

As the sun casts your shadow behind you
As you smile and stand back, aside—
Leaving your hand free to turn, and as I see it now
It gestures in its upturned palm to the sky,
Where we give back each pure moment of our lives.

For Ken Wilber

'Promise me', she said, and you said 'I promise'
I promise I will find you for all time—
And I don't know whose tears they were, yours or mine
As I sit on the grass reading you: but 'Treya died today'
And today is now, and still now, and she is you, and you
And yes, she is in the invisible attuning of our being
Just as you are to me, in your broken heart
And you are, somewhere upstairs in the house—
We are all living and we have all died already
Or our lives are this: a slow unclouding of our love,
Unclothed like flesh

And, Ken, there is you, serving her
And the word *dakini* strangely tapping on my door
All week before I came to this—
And in the uprush, or upwelling, what fills my heart
To say to you is thank you, thank you for reminding us
That this is what love is, and it is real—
This naked *rubedo* with barely words enough to say it
But enough for a liturgy that would shatter like starlight,
Or any human heart—'I promise': and I do

And as I glance up, I see you naked at the window
Waving and smiling down at me in your towel
And then a cluster of starlings fly into the tree beside the border

The evergreen, twenty of them, with a flurry of wings…
And the tree is invisibly full of them singing!
Chock-full of them, squealing and chattering
Their sound and its sweetness, seething
With the woodpigeon on the phone line nearby as a sentinel,

And Treya has just died, and yet everything is magical
The grass—the trees—the sky, everything
As a passing butterfly lands beside me here
And a greenfinch swings on a column of nuts
You'd put out for him, swivelling into view

As you walk out on to the grass to me, smiling
And I can't speak—you know, or seem to…

Everything is as it was in the beginning
And all it takes is to say 'I will'.

Angel-Whisper

for the invisible ones

Trust us as we breathe in you
Trust us as we sense in you—
We walk with you behind your skin
In a shivering which betrays our presence:

We already know you. We have been you.
Only the light in your blood is the difference
And is your becoming, as you become us.

We haunt you as you haunt us—
Caring for what we have seen and known,
And our wings are your arms, but we are not as you imagine
Or as you walk now, you can feel our standing

In the spread of your shoulders, sensing...

And our whisper is like the breeze in the leaves
And the birdsong that pauses you in its pausing,
And it is the whisper of that breeze in you
Where you walk, suddenly in knowing
As its cloak of light gathers around you

And where you come into the mystery in the middle of a field
Without knowing where or why your steps are leading you,
All we see is in you, as your eyes scan the ground
And in the space we leave you
As we surround each moment
True to its unfolding...

And as you come to what you find
That is always your wandering in God,
That is the Body of the Ground
Giving you the secrets of your being

Where the ground streams on
Into the ether of your dreaming...

Where you walk beyond your body
And the shells of your names.

A New Version of the Lord's Prayer

from the Aramaic, after Neil Douglas-Klotz

Great Father-Mother in the light
Sacred in our hearts as Your Name becomes
May Your Oneness come—
Your Desire be done
On earth as it is in the realms above

Give us the bread and the seeing we need
And heal us of our hurtfulness as we release
Those who weave the web against us;

Don't let the world fool us—
And free us from wrong-doingness

For Yours is the fertile field, the I am, and the Great Song

From aeon to aeon
Ameyn: we promise.

~

The Wisdom Tree

Haiku 1

Anglo-Haiku

The green earth:
Does it reach your eyes?
The lambs scatter from the passing train.

Summer Haiku

To think simply
Of you and I sleeping
So close and yet so far.

Listen to the bird's song
Free to one another
Fearless of company.

Dream Haiku

Runes on the table...
Golden secret shadows
Dustfall from the moon.

Irish Haiku

Driving with Catherine
Through Tipperary—
Eating ice cream and reading John Donne.

from the
I Ching (the hexagram cycle)

11   泰   *T'ai*   BENEVOLENCE

The Water Carrier

The breeze blows from T'ai Chi—in the mountain
Ch'ien and K'un are together in you,
Sun and moon—man and woman,
She is in you and you are in her
Your beginning is with you again—
The blessing of the air is like a globe of pearl between you,

And along the dusty road, as the story has it
A man comes into your village carrying water
As he greets you silently, his blue eyes shining,
With the sky wrapped like a cloak around him, behind him,

As he hands it to you.

27   頤   *I*   NOURISHMENT

Eating the Book

Mouthfuls of pages:
Do you know what it is to eat these words?
Then it's not just food you are chewing
But wisdom that can touch your blood
And slake your thirst, and calm your hunger
—your hunger is for what comes first.

Ch'i of your understanding,
And the energy around you it energizes, brightening—

The oracle says: mouthful of teeth, and book:
Be moved by what nurtures you, and through it,
Be open to what is given—

                  this writing

Its marrow made flesh, and the flesh is you.

32 恆 *Heng*   CONSTANCY

To the End of the Heart

It is a long way over the land
It is a long way over the shifting sands
And everything can change, and will—

But there is one thing that can stay
And that is your heart

                always walking under you

Always breathing, always beating inside of you—

And now it says: take it to the limit
—full-blown, like a spinnaker, in front of you—
And it will be taken, and tested,
Touched, transfigured, stretched and tormented

Until you know its meaning is real,

             is All.

37 家人 *Chia Jen* THE CLAN

Shaman Woman

Come home. Listen to the woman now
Listen to her calm, her knowing
—let go to her.

She knows the inside of you
And she knows you belong together.
She knows what binds you—
The whole of her body is that. Listen now.

It is her voice you need to hear
Her benison, her blessing
That stills the air around you

      as she looks into her palms

And the curving grass, the sky and the darting birds
Are one with you—
As you feel the ground beneath your feet
As you gather in, and wait:

      And now is the circle.

41 損 *Sun* GIVING OUT

Giving It

Give out the gift, pour it out like a wound,
Give blood, bone and sinew—
Give love and strength, give it all you have,
And it will return to you:
Your emptiness will be filled.

The gift is for giving—don't hold it back
You can't be a miser and live

But give it mindfully, give it as gold
Glimmering, keening insight, grace
Don't hold back the gift, but the giver
The difference is purity, is this—
Get yourself out of the way…

And then it is not your desire, but its
That gave you the gift to give.

47 困 *K'un* CONSTRICTION

Boundaries

A tree surrounded by a boundary:
You need to enclose your kingdom.

But you don't want to hear it !

You need to make a fortress of where you are
Even as you yearn to go further
On and on over the known world expanding

I can only tell you—you can't.

This is the earth you are on.

Come to ground with what you have
Or else you'll be surrounded—

And if you know what your limits are,
You will use them to anchor your strength.

48 井 *Ching* THE WELL

The Deep Centre

And within this

the centre that is invisible

the well that the fields surround—

And that is invisible in you
Until you learn to be still,

Being like it.
Close your eyes.

Don't move, it says
Go inside,
Breathe down.

See it, now
Deepening into you
Down your throat
And into your belly.

Can you reach it?
Does your rope stretch?
Can you hold it there?

It was always here
It will always stay—
With its deep dark water.

Taste it.

50 鼎 *Ting*   THE SACRIFICE

Offering Up

And can you let it go?
Can you let it be beyond you?
Can you offer it up?

It is hidden in your heart, and your heart knows
This is the sacrifice, and you are it.

Feel it. And it is burning
With the clear flame we call love
That burns off what doesn't belong to it.

Feel it, and it is a jewel
It is the most precious thing you have.

And it is yours—because you gave it.

The flame burns rose in your mind, like wine.

It is the best you have, and you gave it. Can you?

53 漸 *Chien*   COASTING

Rolling

The wagon rolls,
The rock has been entered

    —we're coasting on the freeway—

And teach your soul
How to fly
From the bird
  as it floats on the thermals

To flow with the wind, like water—
Like the movement of your body as you walk at ease
In step with yourself and your feet
Or as you run and feel the breeze on your face,
Free now
                the sea drifting like a great mirror

                its waves rippling, dreaming…

Not forcing the hand of anything
Or of her, as she lies with you now
Your will, or her desire—
And then it is all open, all breathing

        and this is the New Life tao.

55 豐 *Feng*   SOVEREIGNTY

The King

Harvest time now. Bleached light on the fields
And the whole earth gathered in plenty—
Imagine the abundance, it is yours,
You have enough. You can breathe.

The cup is full of wine as you raise it,
Above it are two sheaves of corn…
Now this is the apex, this is the throne
To stand in what is royal in you—

The light everywhere, to your left and right,
The sun still on its wheel of fire,
All flame become light, and the light, gold
So you know the glory that is I
                                for a moment

Where you stand beyond time as you close your eyes

And all you know is the blazing gold
That fills you, reaching down to your feet
And fusing the ground with the sky

And it is not your will, or mine.

56  *Lu*   THE TRAVELLER

After Li Po

Where do you come from? Where are you going?
It is not the world as you see it—
I have different eyes from yours

And I cross your path like a shadow.
What is it you really want?
What is that weight round your shoulders?
Who gave you that complacent smile?

I know a different kind of kingdom
Where all I carry is the sky and the moment
And people are as they are, like me,
And birds and bees and flowers are equal.

Fool, minstrel, tramp—I am all of these
But my secret is I am no one
And the breeze that blows through me is the breeze
And my vanishing breath on the wind.

What I give, I give. It is all I have—
And the miracle is that it's enough.

58 兌 *Tui*   DELIGHT

Sing Out

Open the window to that music
It's catching the beat inside your body
In spite of you, isn't it?

Sun, moon, mountain, kingfisher-moment:
It's all for our delight,
                            didn't you know?

Trust where the line breaks
The mould breaks
And where your energy wants to go—

Have you ever seen an oracle get up and dance?
Well, you have now.

62 小過 *Hsiao Kuo*   THE SMALL THINGS

Down to Size

The lark soars
                and plummets, free-falls,

Landing alert with his head up—

And it's the small things that matter supremely
Which come to meet you on your path.

Do you ignore the tiny desert flower?
Are you a hero treading on a snail?

I tell you, in the end, it is life that matters
In each moment of your responding—
Life, and love: not power.

We've had enough of all that now.

And all the long road into the future is this:
Can you live as if everything mattered?

Then you will live.

from the
Kuan Yin (the 100 quatrains)

for Lucy Lidell

5 In the darkness

Dig deep into the earth where the spring water gushes,
Through sheer pain and labour, seek to win through—
In a place like this, then, you come across a true friend...
And seeing each other again (*it's you!*) you both touch Heaven.

21 Together

The Ultimate and Heaven together make the yin-yang way,
And the melding of man and woman is joyously the same—
So the dragon shall coil and twist with the snake...
And together they shall come into the same dreaming Garden.

34 Morality

In everything you do, live for the truth—
Your words should be clear and your actions substantial,

Don't have ideas in your heart that are not discernible,
Stand at the centre like the bright rays pouring from the sun!

48 Wisdom

Heaven below zero, the earth freezing, water congealing
So what is the point of being famous and well known?
It's best to wait and see beyond all of this—
Until the real time comes, and your eye can see clearly.

60 Inferno

The fire swells with heat when it's stoked up with fuel,
It ravages a tract of land—and then it turns on you,
It's no use; you're going to burn in your own blood,
Do you think your money can buy you out?

74 Being Who You Are

A snow goose snags itself inside a cage—
Wanting to change itself, this is *not* the way through
Every way *away from herself* she can't escape…
This reading is the saddest and truest one of all.

85 Awakening

The clouds part, but the way is misty on the mountain:
All of Creation becomes a circle when the moon is full—
When you wake up, your fictional dreams and fantasies die,
And the wise one will lead you to the true, real Paradise.

Translated with Man-Ho Kwok and Martin Palmer

from
The Windsor Sequence

at the Faith & Ecology Summit, Windsor Castle, May 1995

Windsor

The castle huge on its mound: here it is
Rising like all of England above the town—
Its grey walls as if made of a different substance:

A haunting set in impenetrable stone

Crowds of day-trippers wandering, hanging around
The air primed as if for a festival
As if something momentous was about to happen:

And it never does

And nothing can stop us wanting it to
Needing a royalty we know in our blood
That takes our steps reaching up—
Not draining down the endless Saturday arcade

'Hey, photograph me with Queen Victoria!'
Waves the old U.S. soldier in his green beret
Grinning from ear to ear where she holds her sceptre, down

There on the island with the pavement-side staring, uncaring
And inside the gate, past the friendly bobby
It's real enough as suddenly a make believe guardsman
Screams at a lad to step back over the line—

Screams with all the pain of being a machine
Faithful to a Lady who is nowhere to be found

from

Welcomes

after the Venerable Kushok Bakula

Your bowed, bared shaven head—
Deep-set cheeks and sunken, all-seeing eyes…
At the very moment you thought you were free to retire—
You had to take on the whole burden of your world
Like a cross, there, on your shoulders:

Bodhisattva.

How many of you are willing to lose your names?

Then yours will be the Shining Throne

—the true place of light where you are seated, within.

Buddhism

after the Venerable Kushok Bakula

'We all drink the same water of life', you say
With your quiet all-suffering, seeing face
Interpreted into our language—

And the leather brown of the earth of your skin
That is the contact of skin with the ground

Eyes that have seen all,
That know the pain and illusions we create,
And have let them go…to the earth and the sky

And isn't *this* tradition:
To return to what is alive
To what has always been here?

So you named the mountain 'Ratna Peak'
You adjured abstention and compassion there—
And as you pause on the pass, in our eyes
You pray and ask forgiveness from it:

And the mountain is Divine.

And on the plains below, once tyranny* had collapsed—
The true faith grew up like flowering weeds, everywhere.

* Stalinism in Mongolia

Judaism

after Rabbi Arthur Hertzberg

'Three Jews, three opinions'—you laugh
Out of your modesty, relaxing the tension,
As the gift of your humour warms the air

And then the joke's on you, as your glasses
Slip briefly off your nose—
As you turn to gravity, to what matters here

And in that brief nakedness of your eyes
Everything you say resonates as it needs to, now

'Animals were not created to serve Man,
Nothing in Creation was created to serve Man,
We must change...'
As the green herb of Genesis drifts back
As you talk of the root we have ravaged and plucked
In the forests of our lungs and our breathing—

'To create the land of milk and honey again
That the Bible so warmly promises...'

—oh song of songs, of flesh with flesh
And flower with grass and stone, as one,
Song of Songs sung into the wound—

Into the rape of our desecration…and now?

As you say it, it's not looking above, below, or back
But forward, into the sacred sign
You trace between your mouth and your finger, raised

In a language so like Deaf and Dumb.

Islam

after Professor Muhammed Hyder

Your God of the Absolute
In His searching blazing desert light
Is nowhere to be found over your head:
Your presence is here, and your warmth is deep,
And as broad as your shoulders in its embrace:

Soul, we called it, remember?
In your patient ear like a mountain
And in the slow rooted movement of your speech

But let's be practical: you number the trees
Replanted with drip irrigation—
You talk of cleaning water, and organic farming,
As you ask 'How can we reach the millions worldwide?'

And let's be real: what blocks out the light?
Those with their axes to grind—and those that deny
That 'daily bread doesn't exist for most of these people'
As we sit, well-fed, in this tasteful library
Not one of us starving, or only of heart—

And that is the truth beyond our minds
Old Grandfather Adam, as you spell it:
This Oneness, this Allah is all over the ground
Calling our names out loud.

from

Tantrika
the songs of the Sixth Dalai Lama

for Lucy, again

1.

Over the eastern ridge rises
The white face of the moon;
In my mind emerges
The smiling mouth of my beloved.

9.

Enamoured of the lake
The swan longs to linger,
But the ice covers the water
And the swan leaves no regrets.

11.

I have hung up prayer flags
For the good luck of my beloved
Keeper of forests, *Ajo Shelngo*
Don't trample her fragile colours.

13.

The legal stamp to seal documents
Can't say a thing in evidence
It's better to imprint your own heart
With the hallmark of truth and justice.

21.

She flashed her smile
At the crowd in the tavern,
But from the corner of her eyes
She told me her love for me.

31.

From childhood, my beloved
Seems to have come from the wolf's race,
Even after all these nights, she tries
To escape like them, to the hills.

43.

Even the stars can be measured:
Her body can be caressed—
Oh yes, but you'll never reach the bottom
Of the depth of her hidden yearnings.

50.

She left with her cocked hat
Shaking her hair back
Saying goodbye to me—
'It's sad to say goodbye,' I said
'Don't be sad, dear one,' she replied
'After every parting we can meet again.'

55.

The willow's in love with the sparrow
And the sparrow feels the same
When the willow and sparrow love each other
What can the grey hawk do about it?

Based on literal versions by K Dhondup, Dharamsala, India, 1981

Couplet

after a reading in Lisbon

'It's not *all* love', she said
No, but it is in the end.

from
Rosa Mundi

for Z.

In love there is a fire, and in the fire there is a flame. And in the flame there is another who has known us before time. She knows him now, he knows her name. And it's in the face behind our faces, the voice inside our voices, where light gathers at our edges as our eyes meet again.

And she can stretch him to the edges of his life. And he can take her into the depth of her fire.

And who are they? The ones who have agreed to love, to open each other to the quick and the core of their being.

And so his eyes can see her as she is, and her hands can know him as he is. And the seeing and the knowing is in them and beyond them like a star. They are following a dancing flame into the darkness that is daylight, reading the signs inside out and learning to trust. Because what they live is in matter, but it is light. It is light; but not even their love can fathom it. And it moves, as it breathes, with its own life.

So she is one and many, as she is woven in herself, one and many as we all are dancing together; one by one for the journey that is love, lover by lover that is stardust, flesh-grass and stone.

We are all lovers in the Rose.

Haiku 2

Heaven

We live in hands of light
That are not hands—
But an edge we cannot see.

Earth

It's wonderful to think
Of such a long river
With no words in it.

Kinsale

Salt harbour air
The scent of longing—
The sea nowhere in sight.

Rhyader

The sky breaking
Between light and shadow:
Foxgloves under the scree.

Dream Haiku 2

Trust 'I know'—
Trust 'I like'—
Trust the doors of night.

Inside Out

Anos de Amigos, 1996

the prediction

'Anos de amigos!', he announces—and now a line
Of brightly coloured discs pressed close: all our faces
Like in a long school photograph, transformed into colour
Each of us individual, none of us separate or divided—
Ruby, orange, blue, crimson…hazed into their textures,
And in the shade of each, you can see our depth:

And we are friends here, not couples anymore: we are family,
We are brothers and sisters to the core, each one of us alone,
And each of us is a circle—a free child grown whole…

Triptych

The Day

for Jane

Like a great crystal where you could see forever
Across the white expanse of the frosted fields—
And the sunlight and the frost-light were one light
Under the pale blue vast void Heaven of the sky
That blended into the farthest reaches of the land
Miraculously at its edge…and was full again

'As if the whole landscape has become transparent', I said
—translucent in its whitened ground and mist—
And you replied, from behind the wheel
'It's as if the light is coming up out of the ground'
So we were balanced in the scales, Above and Below

And in the after-echo of what you'd said
That I wrestled with and doubted

(As only a man can doubt a woman)
Suddenly, the plunge—
Out of eyesight, and deeper than insight
To see the earth's own inner sun rising to meet its other—yes

Where the circle is completed, and we are one...

The Hour

1.

Can you hear the stars calling?
Can you hear their ringing sound?

From inside all the worlds, for a moment
Beyond the walls, and all illusion

Where they conjunct, fusing
At the centre of your skull

2.

For two minutes, pure seething sound
Then a a clarity as if from behind the eyes,
Waking inwardly to see in calm

Buddhas of statuesque stillness, unveiled

3.

A pregnancy like stone
Surly, the grey day
Narrowed to a point:

We have to go beyond this bubble of our minds.

Aren't you sick of endless half-thoughts?

I could shake my head
As if surrounded by mosquitoes
For some stillness–to penetrate beyond

To let the pure moment in

4.

The truth that is wordless
Will detonate our words
Exploding their husks
From the inside out

Until all that is left
In the fallen detritus
Is pure naked meaning

note: 'The Hour' describes a particular conjunction of major planets that on the astrological grid formed a perfect Star of David on 23.1.97 at 5.30pm

The Moment

for Norman Jope

After all night sleepless again (how many of us?)
The circle threatening its closure in darkness
Under the burning white lens of the moon—
And the wailing sirens, police or ambulance, or both
Whirling, still crazily loudening and fading

As the first bird in the still-dark, suddenly
Fills the whole space of the blackened window
With a song clearer and more limpid
Than any flute, than dripping silver water

Than a string of similes...

With a song born of a man
With an invisible shaded instrument
Who has spent the whole night
Waiting in silence:
And you can believe it—
These are his first words

His wisdom finally
As vulnerable as a heartbeat
Hammered in the breath,

And it is the dawn–
We have weathered it.

Grace will come
Rarer than any death,
Suddener than swan-white snow...

He stands where the circle would have closed.

In the Church of the Heart

at the Ucheldre Centre, Holyhead

There has been a quiet, long revolution
For centuries of anaemic suffering
And now we have taken over the building.

It is the Sabbath, and we are working.

A pale sun streams through the stained glass slits,
The tables have been overturned, and piled neatly
And the chairs everywhere are red

Like the curtained altar above the steps

And there is no priest or liturgy,
Only three women and a man
Spread out between the cloisters and the congregation

With pens in our hands, writing, listening, feeling

For this red hour
That is our communion,
Before we come to each other for confession...

As the wind lifts and breaks outside, like a flooding sea.

In a Zen Garden

for Rupert Loydell, who suggested it

Lifting the latch
Of the black bamboo lych gate
Into the present moment of buried boulders,
A *zendo* like a transformed bus-shelter fronting
Raked, grey-white gravel as delicate
As planted furrows

The smallness of an exotic tree peeping through
With its mucus leaves and red berries dangling
Privet, ponticum and pine among the rocks
And other seedling bushes and shrubs
To bring our eyes down to detail:

And over the wall from the other culture
Pink blossom hangs effusive as uncut hair
Over the gun-metal green ivy under it,
And the conifer tree leaning over this side wall...

But the birds sing, careless of boundaries,
And as piercing as pins in the after-rain—
And the wind that sweeps over our seeing and listening
Where being here is all that being is
As it fills our eyes, and empties.

~

Cirrus,
        blue sky,
                red tipped leaves
And falling—

How come these tiny shrubs
Feel as if they have been so loved
That the eyes that have seen them
Become ours as we look at them?

~

No breath, no body
Neither of them mine now

Only a hollow presencing
That is as real as the stones
Present to themselves
Without knowing it

Or knowing themselves
As divorced, as their own.

Nothing breathes, nothing is
Outside of Is
That we
Have called God

And which I
Call You...

Three notes behind me, on a bassoon

As the whole air moves on into music,
And the tread of a student's footsteps, passing.

~

I am a drunk here
Sleeping on a bench
In Paradise Garden

Listening to birdsong
Listening to music
Listening to wind

As they mix in my blood
And flood with a sudden warmth that is
No one's, into joy.

~

My mind drifts—or my thinking
Then a single door slamming somewhere shut like a shotgun

And a seagull, calling…

~

Be here.
Be dressed by the wind.

Undressed by the wind.

Your hair combed through,
Your eyes clearing
Breakfasting on breath…

Be here
From the beginning.

~

Two jackdaws drifting in flight,
Two more passing them

Now the air is full of their clacking colloquy...

And below, in the gravel field,
Are all the seeds of silence you will ever need.

~

So fast, so soon, so like a dream
As the wind rises in a gust, and the cough
That suddenly catches in your throat
With an *Oh*, like a realization

Becomes the inaudible bell
And the clappers of wood
Announcing that the period
                              is over.

~

from

like lightning inside lightning

for Rupert Loydell

'Dust you are—
And to dust you shall return'
He is saying
And then the touch of his finger
Drawing the cross
On our foreheads, one by one

And as we queue in a shaft of late evening sun
All dying, in this fragile standing flesh—
All so transient, so fleeting,

That the only thing that matters
Is what we are, in what we do:

Conduct is everything,
And this is our chance

The rest is nothing
The rest is a dying

To what can stand in the light
Receiving this ashen sign…
And shine,
                    as it does

Knowing it has been touched,
Knowing the silent miracle—

That it is not dust.

~

for Luce

No spell can hold
Beside the truth—
No distance can be sustained
Beside your face

This is how we will meet, and be met
With the shock of your spreading
Rooted-to-the-spot smile

Where lightning becomes love,
Gratitude, secret relief and laughter

The way it is in Heaven—

The way it is where lightning lives
In the place we call *ever after.*

In the bar below deck
As the light dims outside
Past twilight into a foreboding
Inky blue-black murk—
Like rain or thunder, or worse

Broken only by the occasional
Crest of a white wave—

We talk, the three of us
And there is our light
As invisibly

Until it glows, caught
In the mirror of the heart
Like a palpable warmth
Around every softening edge

Where a pregnant woman standing
In the regal darkness of her hair
Has it

And the Polish woman at the cafeteria till
Of this Greek boat sailing across the Irish Sea
Has it

And we have it as we walk out into the breeze—
With the sea like the world slipping past under us

And what is it? I want to call it love
But it is more natural even than words

What it does comes closer:
   Accepting everything as it is
      So that everything becomes it.

~

Above the winding silken river
With its pair of drifting swans
Spread blanket you have brought
And uncorked cool white wine

It's familiar enough
Romantic stuff—no ?
But it's not what we are saying

It's not the woman you are
Talking about the pain
Of being adored and expected from
But not seen as you are
As another struggling soul

And nor is it
What suddenly comes over
This man you are with
As you tell him you're jaded with his kind

And he jumps—he springs
At you like a playful tiger—
Rolling you both breathless
Twenty foot down the grassy bank…
Where you lie for a moment, laughing
And then strangely shy

This isn't the story it set out to be—
This is tearing the veil where no camera can enter

Until we are ready
To tell you
How it is to be
A man and a woman, equally

And how love is itself
When it is—
And is nothing else.

Maitreya

If you came now
How would you seem?
How would you walk?

Huge, transparent
Through the battlefield
Of the present—

Sad as you were then,
As the firing passes
Through your seamless garment

But to all who recognize you
A welling joy, and a greeting
As you spread your arms:
Do you?

Or has life
Become so complicated
That the light can no longer condense
Into a single human figure
And surround it?

Or is it simply
(As it always was)
That we were looking the other way
For a saviour in our own image;
Condemning you to invisibility again?

Teach us, Lord
How we are you—
Man, woman, child
Animal, tree and stone—

If we choose to be.

I told you
We knew it
We know it
Don't we?

It will go on
Until this carapace
Around our hearts
Is broken free

By any means
As lyrical or absurd
As two trains meeting

In their sleep.

~

for Marion

Thinking of what
I'd been told
As you told me
What you'd told her

I see you telling the truth
And the truth is light
And your light touches
The light in her

Like that—light to light

So that even if she
Or they aren't aware
Even if they don't
Speak the language

They know—and we're through

Light to light
　　　　　beyond words, beyond worlds

Where we stand
In truth

　　　　　　　　　～

　　　　　for Dawn

　　　You dancer
　　　With your belly of fire
　　　Liquid as the dance
　　　Being poured into itself—

　　　You move like lava
　　　Under your flaming hair
　　　And cool silk skirt
　　　　　　　　you hitch
　　　To the wagon of your star

　　　And calling us forward,
　　　You presence us,
　　　Breathe us and free us

　　　Where we gather like a wave,
　　　Where you are the shore

　　　And you are the wave's height
　　　Rising to its wildest—
　　　Returning to its slowing
　　　　　　　　　stillness

　　　All in the mere shape of you
　　　And the space you give
　　　Out of your womb
　　　Spanning the earth with yourself
　　　Like a miraculous thread

　　　Of heaven-sent sense

for Jenny

No separation—
This is the dance in heaven
Where we are all connected
As we want to be

No preference either
You can move freely
The way you orbit the room mercurially

Encompassing us all—

And as we glance
In and out of each other's smiling
No fear: as you tiger-dance playfully
Into my space: your white smocking gyrating
Above your black-strapped boots as you pass

As close as you want to
Before moving on again—

No fear, and no holding
In the light around your eyes
That says we are not defined by this
But only by a different understanding

So that when we finally breathe close,
As the music slows,
                              we breathe
With nothing between us but the fullness
Of all we have felt, in every cell—
Belly to belly

No separation

(But how can I tell you
How it is in heaven?

You need to go there yourself, and see

Leaving your ego outside with the doorman,
Letting your mind go into your feet)

~

for S.

What is it that can reach us
Not as flesh but light

The way you come to me
Across the air

Shining into my inner skin,
So that everything you touch
Is closer even than your body
Could be to me now

Inside my skin and inside each cell
Where there is light
Like a miraculous undiscovered cave
Deep inside the earth

That is the heart's,
                    secretly
Behind everything—

In what moves, breathes, dances and is still

Revealing us as we are, unmasked

And here, miles apart, where we're
Both sun and moon, brother and sister to each other
And neither–

Mutually eclipsed in light

Becoming something lighter still,
As new as it is other.

~

for Kathleen Raine

Your plain black hardback cover
With its gold lettered spine
Beside this week's cover of *Time Out*
With its loud blonde majorette shouting cheers!
Like a diminutive clown—

Distracting me, and you
And with the transient
Beside the permanent
It's like this: which do we choose?
And for how long?

I'll just wait before I walk to the Holy Mountain
You think, but then two hours have passed
Like your life.

And it's getting late, too late
And all you can do is sleep
The sleepwalk of regret

The grey dawn that becomes a whole day

When out of nowhere in the void
A voice keeps saying
'Lose what you're doing
Come back to the path

Forgiveness, reconnection, blessing
Is instant if you can choose it—
Grasp the golden wire.'

~

Latifa

Dappled leaves in the sunlight or the rain
The river snaking brightly through the trees below
And with the wind, streaming like the sea.

The river in all its moods, rising and falling

The breeze giving way to stillness as I go on breathing

The sun and its absence in grey clouded shadow

And a great calm descends.

Just think how long you spent
Wanting me to be other than I was.

Quatrain

for Susie

'To really be breathed through
By the rightness of each moment—
That would be living in the light...'
'That would be living', you replied.

Postscript:
The Bell

Ask not for whom the bell tolls...

What is that sound
Echoing on the air
That calls us in the wind?

What is it that rings
In its soft whispering tolling
Heard between the waves
Or as the air breathes, rolling

On a green marker buoy, swaying—
Or in a quiet Irish garden
Pausing between steps
About to be taken...

What is this
Church of the air
That has no walls

Calling us to what moves
Beyond the moving world?

And is it to dying
Or to life—when we
Don't know the time for either?

There is no answer:
There is only its haunting
Ghost echo that brings us
Into the soul of its sound

Like a mantra
Without a singer
That has one unpronounceable

Word it spells, over and over
Or an invisible knowing
That says
You are watched over
And we know all
Your coming and going
Your beginning and your end

And is it that
Which secretly thrills
Making you feel
So suddenly transparent
That there is nowhere to hide
And everything is in the mystery?

Where a ringing bell at sea
Or here, as unexpectedly
Is enough to remind you
Of all you need to be
And believe

And know
Of what is first and foremost
And has always been
From before the beginning?

Listen. Can you hear it ringing,
Deep in the centre
Behind your thinking?

Listen, listen well.
Listen, listen, listen well.

Acknowledgements

Acknowledgements are due to the following magazines and journals in which some of these poems first appeared:

Only Poetry, Jungle (Paris), *The Moorland Review, Island* (Athens), *Strange Mathematics, Apart* (Dusseldorf), *Reality Studios, Parallel* (Brussels), *City Limits, The Green Book, Stride, Acumen, Rustic Rub, Resurgence, Kindred Spirit, Memes, 3X4, Terrible Work, Wavelength* (Lisbon), *The Weaver* (HarperCollins internet magazine), *Touchstone* (the Order of Bards, Ovates & Druids), *Otter, Unicorn, Acid Rainbow Dada Dance, Tears in the Fence, Seam* and *Fire.*

'Dark of a Dream', 'Club Monte Solaire' and 'To the Swan' appeared in *Angels of Fire – an anthology of radical poetry in the 80s* (Chatto & Windus, 1986); *The White Poem*, with photographs by Carole Bruce, was first published by Five Seasons Press/Rivelin Grapheme Press (1988); 'New Age' appeared in *Transformation – the poetry of spiritual consciousness* (Rivelin Grapheme, 1988); 'By the Shores of Loch Awe' in *With My Heart in My Mouth* (Rudolf Steiner Press, 1994); 'into the heart: for Gillian' in *Earth Ascending – an anthology of living poetry* (Stride, 1997) and 'from transmissions' in *Most This Amazing Day* (Fount, 1998).

'Adam's Song' was set to music by composer Rosemary Duxbury on our cassette album *Thread of Gold* (1992) along with 'Canticle to the Sun' (from The Paradiso Drafts, 4.). The full orchestral version of 'Canticle to the Sun' was first performed at Quorn, near Leicester and sung by tenor Christopher Martyn.

'You are a River and a Rose' was broadcast on BBC Three Counties Radio as part of an interview with Simon Price (1995); and *Strange Days* formed a part of the text of Martin Palmer's Easter programme for Radio 4 'There is a Green Hill' (1996).

Thanks are also due to The Diamond Press, Victoria Press, Rivelin Grapheme Press, Five Seasons Press, Stride Publications, Element Books, HarperCollins, Icorec/Arc and the University of Salzburg for permission to reprint poems from my various collections.

Special thanks to the following without whom this book would not have come into being: Sylvia Paskin, Geoffrey Godbert, Carole Bruce, Snowdon Barnett, Kim and Barrie Simpson, Glenn Storhaug, Rupert Loydell, Jehanne Mehta, Lady Bronwen Astor, Gabriel Bradford Millar, Jenny Davis, Marion Fawlk, Susan Mears (my agent), Martin Palmer and Icorec, Lucy Lidell, Bob Moore (in Denmark), Marion Shiel (in Ireland), Carolyn Finlay and my Chrysalis students, Catherine Abbott, Lindsay and Phoebe Clarke, Donna Salisbury, Zanna Beswick, Maggie Peters, Jane Routh, Kathleen Raine, Ann Meek, Susie Nott Bower, Florence Hamilton (my editor) and Michael Mann (my publisher). We are all interwoven so much more deeply than we know.

J.R.

List of Titles and Sources

Titles of Poems and Sources

Prelude: from *Psychic Poetry – a manifesto* (1984)

Action (*The Opening*, 1980)
Dark of a Dream (*The Opening*, 1980)
Ystradafellte (*The Opening*, 1980)
Aloneness (*The Opening*, 1980)
Club Monte Solaire (*The Hole*, 1982)
The Beach (*The Hole*, 1981)
Utterance (*The Hole*, 1983)
Writing on Air (*The Hole*, 1983)
Light (*The Hole*, 1982)
To the Swan (*The Hole*, 1982-3)
from *In the Valley of Shadow* (1981-6)
from *transmissions* (1984-6)
Into the Depth (*Divinations*, 1984)
Knowing (*Divinations*, 1985)
Notation (*Divinations*, 1985)
The White Poem (*Divinations*, 1985)
Beginning (*Divinations*, 1985)
Sophia (*Divinations*, 1986)
from *Trwyn Meditations* (1986)
from *New Age* (*Divinations*, 1987)
Summa (*Heart of Earth*, 1986)
from Glastonbury Triptych (*Heart of Earth*, 1986)
A Fresh Blue Message (*Heart of Earth*, 1988)
from into the heart (*Heart of Earth*, 1989)
Humility (*Heart of Earth*, 1986)
Forgetting (*Heart of Earth*, 1988)
from A Bridge of Dreams (*Heart of Earth*, 1988)
from borderlines (*Heart of Earth*, 1988)
from By the Shores of Loch Awe (*Heart of Earth*, 1989)
Given (*Strange Days*, 1990)
from The Paradiso Drafts (*Journey to Eden*, 1991)
The Room (*Heart of Earth*, 1990)
from *For Now* (1990)
from *Pilgrimage* (1993-4)
Adam's Song (*Improvisations*, 1990)
Owl (*Heart of Earth*, 1990)
Lines in Any Season (*Heart of Earth*, 1990)
Transience (*Heart of Earth*, 1991)

For Thomas Merton (*Heart of Earth*, 1991)
Hawthorn, Blackthorn (*Heart of Earth*, 1991)
Day of the Star (*Heart of Earth*, 1991)
The Stone (*Heart of Earth*, 1991)
It Goes On (Chiron III) (*Heart of Earth*, 1991)
You are a River and a Rose (*Heart of Earth*, 1991)
from the *Tao Te Ching* (1991)
On an Icon of St. John (*Heart of Earth*, 1991)
Mother Song (Uncollected, 1991)
Prayer at Sheepscombe (Uncollected, 1992)
Fragment on Swift's Hill (*Heart of Earth*, 1992)
Koan (Uncollected, 1992)
from *Stories Beyond Words* (1992)
In the End: the Beginning (*Meditations on the Unknown God*, 1993)
from *At Glasshampton Monastery* (*Meditations on the Unknown God*, 1993)
Through the Wicklow Gap (*Meditations on the Unknown God*, 1993)
from At Cortijo Romero (*Meditations on the Unknown God*, 1993)
The Way Through (*Meditations on the Unknown God*, 1993)
For Ken Wilber (*Meditations on the Unknown God*, 1993)
Angel-Whisper (*Meditations on the Unknown God*, 1993)
A New Version of the Lord's Prayer (*Meditations on the Unknown God*, 1994)
Haiku 1 (Uncollected, 1988-94)
from the *I Ching – the hexagram cycle* (1994)
from *Kuan Yin – the 100 quatrains* (1994)
from *The Windsor Sequence* (1995)
from *Tantrika:* the songs of the Sixth Dalai Lama (1996)
Couplet (*Uncollected*, 1995)
from *Rosa Mundi* (*Alchemy – the art of transformation*, 1995-6)
Haiku 2 (Uncollected, 1994-8)
Anos de Amigos, 1996 (*Midnight Silver*, 1997)
Triptych (*Midnight Silver*, 1997)
In the Church of the Heart (*Midnight Silver*, 1997)
In a Zen Garden (Uncollected, 1997)
from *like lightning inside lightning* (1997-8)
Latifa (*Out of this World*, 1998)
Quatrain (Uncollected, 1998)

Postscript: The Bell (Uncollected, 1997)

Published Works

Psychic Poetry – a manifesto (The Diamond Press, 1985).
Now reprinted by Stride Publications and available @£3.50 from 11
Sylvan Road, Exeter, Devon EX4 6EW).

The Opening,Knife in the Light – a stage-poem,The Hole, Bks 1-3 of *The
Great Return* (The Diamond Press, 1988: 2 vol. Standard edition).

In The Valley of Shadow/Divinations, Bks 4-5 of *The Great Return* (The
Diamond Press, 1988: 2 vol. Standard Edition). Some copies of both
still available from Chrysalis at 1 The Mews, Greenhouse Barn,
Greenhouse Lane, Painswick, Glos. GL6 6SE @£14.95 plus £2
postage & packing.

The White Poem, Five Seasons Press, 1988. Some hardback copies still
available from Chrysalis @£12.95

Transformation – the poetry of spiritual consciousness, Rivelin
Grapheme Press, 1988, Afterword by Sir George Trevelyan, available
from Chrysalis @£6.95

Raw Spiritual – selected poems 1980–85, Rivelin Grapheme Press,
1986, available from Chrysalis @£4.95

transmissions (Stride Publications, 1989). *Out of print.*

Trwyn Meditations (Victoria Press, 1986). *Out of print.*

Journey to Eden (with Jenny Davis) (Eden Centre Books, 1991). Some
copies still available @£5.95 from 38 Lee Road, Lynton, North Devon
EX35 6BS.

For Now (with Geoffrey Godbert) (The Diamond Press, 1991).
Available @£6.95 from Chrysalis.

Improvisations (Stride, 1994). Available @£6.95 from Stride, 11
Sylvan Rd, Exeter, Devon EX4 6EW.

Tao Te Ching (Element Books, 1993). Available from Element in
several editions.

Meditations on the Unknown God (University of Salzburg, 1996).
Available @£8.95 from Drake International, Market House, Market
Place, Deddington, Oxford OX15 0SE.

I Ching – the shamanic oracle of change (Thorsons, 1995). Available from HarperCollins.

Kuan Yin – myths and prophecies of the Chinese Goddess of Compassion (Thorsons, 1995). Available from HarperCollins.

Tantrika – Love Songs of the Sixth Dalai Lama (Lung Gom Press, 1996). Available @£1.50 from 2 Henderson St, Kingseat, Dunfermline, Fife KY12 OTP.

Alchemy – the art of transformation (Thorsons, 1997). Available from HarperCollins.

Out of this World (Chrysalis, 1998). Available @£3.50 from Chrysalis.

Further Information

For further information about Jay Ramsay's work and **Chrysalis – the poet in you**, with its unique two-part correspondence course, workshops around the UK, on-going writing groups, and one-to-one creative, therapeutic and healing sessions in London and Gloucestershire, please contact: The Secretary, Chrysalis, 1 The Mews, Greenhouse Barn, Greenhouse Lane, Painswick, Glos. GL6 6SE with an A5 stamped self-addressed envelope and your postal and telephone/fax details.